How to Manage with a Magic Wand

(No, Don't Hit Your
"Problem Employees" over the Head with It!)

Helen M. Thamm, APRN, CPC

WestBow
PRESS
A DIVISION OF THOMAS NELSON

ISBN: 978-1-4497-2281-4 (e)
ISBN: 978-1-4497-2279-1 (sc)
ISBN: 978-1-4497-2280-7 (hc)
Library of Congress Control Number: 2011912943

WestBow Press books may be ordered through booksellers or by contacting:

WestBow Press
A Division of Thomas Nelson
1663 Liberty Drive
Bloomington, IN 47403
www.westbowpress.com
1-(866) 928-1240

Printed in the United States of America

WestBow Press rev. date: 8/9/2011

Acknowledgments:

I am thankful for the enlightened leaders, some of whose input helped make this book powerful. These knowledgeable professionals effectively shared their expertise in dealing with leadership challenges such as staff conflicts by participating in my nursing leadership issues/challenges survey (Thamm 2009). I would like to especially acknowledge the DON who contributed the quarter system team building activity, which has been embraced enthusiastically by her staff and has helped increase their morale as well.

Introduction

My passion for years has been to help new female managers, especially nurse managers, supervisors, and directors to develop and lead harmonious as well as productive teams. When I was dubbed "the manager with the magic wand, you can get them to do anything", I realized one basic challenge was dealing with the misbelief there actually was a "them." However, I was not what I call a natural born nursing leader. I began my journey much like Chris in the story. I was a caring and dedicated nurse who had been a grass roots leader on an evening shift, before venturing into the politics of daytime managing in a hospital. I loved working with my small PM staff. We all got along well, with a shared mission to give the best patient care possible.

However, when I transitioned to the day shift, I felt like I had traveled to another planet. I was not prepared for the politics, and for having to change my mindset, much like the pie baker in Michael Gerber's *E-myth Revisited* (Gerber 1995), from being mainly a technically expert person into one who had to get the work done through other people. Managing at a middle manager level also had unique challenges. For example, the politics could be brutal on all three shifts I lead, and each had diverse personalities and unique priorities. I was also a member of a peer group with the director of nursing as my immediate supervisor and found a disempowered and an almost apathetic attitude permeated that team. In addition, I was a member of the full management team of the hospital, where I found I had little impact, and felt almost like a child being told what to do by a parent (our CEO).

Due to my early negative introduction into middle management, I developed what I call my RESPECT TEAMS process. Rather than high control and punishment as motivators and viewing staff as merely blocks on a schedule, I created a more humanistic theory. RESPECT TEAMS, you will probably guess, is an acronym of the first letters of each chapter which represent the twelve steps of the process that helped me transform into the "manager with a magic wand." The steps guide leaders to create collaborative rather than competitive teams, taking into consideration staff differences of personality styles, communication modes and age groups, along with their individual needs and fears. They also help leaders develop more sophisticated self assessment and life balance skills so they can become less stressed and more satisfied in their careers as well.

Steps To Becoming The Manager With The Magic Wand:

When Chris—the fictitious novice nurse manager in the story —traveled her bumpy path, she had a salty old guide—Marie, the evening nursing supervisor—gently mentoring her along the way.

Bet you can guess that Marie is actually me. I wish there had been a Marie for me, however, many years ago when I began my nursing leadership journey as that fledgling nurse manager. Unfortunately, my role models actually admonished me for caring about the staff's needs, or for that matter its humanity. I remember being told that I should simply regard staff as blocks on a schedule, and nothing more.

I want the true life based information in this book to help save new nursing and other female leaders from experiencing the pain I endured years ago, and which caused me to resign from my first leadership position after only eight months. Unfortunately, even today in many organizations there may still be few or even no positive coach/mentors who truly understand a humanistic approach to leadership.

When I became a nursing supervisor somewhat later in my career, I luckily met an exceptional supervisor who worked at a similar hospital and who agreed to mentor me for my first year. She showed me how to take a fluid team and grow it into a productive and more harmonious one than the stable teams that worked during the week. In my role as weekend nursing supervisor/off-shift administrator, I was able to meld full time charge nurses who worked every other weekend with part-time charge nurses (and staff) to create a dynamic team. We ran full programs in a psychiatric hospital utilizing only nursing staff (no activity therapy, social workers, etc) and had a lower rate of sick call-offs than during the week, demonstrating great staff satisfaction as well.

I felt compelled to share my success with other people. It seemed so simple that I wondered why more managers had not embraced the concepts I used to develop into the "manager with a magic wand", especially in the nursing field. However, I then realized that most nurses and women in general have not taken classes in management/leadership, and when you learn from others who have learned from their predecessors, the same beliefs or misbeliefs often get passed down. Those misbeliefs foster a misconception that high control—with penalties for not doing things "right"—is the way to lead. However, a more democratic, high respect, low control and high staff input way of leading actually inspires much better cooperation. This style also decreases conflict and work stress and motivates staff members to do their best work.

In the story, Marie helped Chris navigate her first year and supported her in becoming a dynamically successful nurse leader, much as my mentor helped me. She encouraged Chris to assess both team and self at deeper levels, believe in herself, remember to nurture herself, and become more empowered and satisfied in her role.

If you or someone you care about is presently a *Chris* without a *Marie*, it is and has been my purpose for years to help you succeed. You can get the free report, *How to Beat Bully Behavior* at *www.NurseCareerSuccess.com*. If you would like to continue fine tuning your leadership skills, you can also request *Five Steps to Nurse Career Success* as well as ongoing success tips at my website, and can follow me on Twitter at: *nursecareersucc*.

You can reach me personally for questions at: *nursecareersuccess@ rtconnect.net*

Prologue

Chris could feel the dampness at the nape of her neck. She always had problems with sweating in that one spot when she was facing a challenge or starting a new path. *What have I gotten myself into?* she thought as she attempted to walk with confidence onto the nursing unit she had called home for three years. On the evening shift, she had been the charge RN, and aside from Marie, the nursing supervisor, who visited for a few minutes per shift, she was the undisputed leader of her team. Why did she feel so nervous? After all, she was a bachelor's-degree prepared nurse, had been around the nursing field for almost eight years, and knew what she was doing—as a nurse.

Chris was already beginning to wonder if she should have taken on this nurse manager role at all. Although she initially felt honored that she was asked to interview for the job by her former nurse manager and was accepted after only one interview, she had some doubts about accepting it. She was also a little surprised that the director of nursing chose her over a day-shift RN. She knew most promotions to management came from professionals on that shift, even though her former nurse manager had recommended her. She was also warned that she would be taking on a political position, while Chris was still a clinician at heart. Her five-staff member evening team had been together for almost two years and worked so well with each other that Chris felt it was no problem being in charge. Also, if anything problematic did happen, she could call Marie, the evening nursing supervisor, and ask her to help brainstorm or problem-solve with her. Now she felt alone.

Chris forced a smile as she passed through her thirty-bed nursing unit and went into morning report. It was difficult for her not to start taking notes about each patient, as she had done for so long in anticipation of making out a staff assignment. The permanent day charge nurse was doing this instead. Chris knew this day charge nurse would be a challenge, as Darlene had applied for the job that Chris received. Chris noted a smug look on Darlene's face. This did not help her feel any more confident about taking over her new position. However, Chris continued to sit with both feet on the floor and her hands on her armrests, trying to emulate the Abe Lincoln power posture. She thought it would help her at least look like a powerful leader, even if her confidence level did not match that ideal. Chris remained quiet, trying to assess the situation. That first encounter seemed to last forever, and she felt relieved when the report was over.

The next day, Chris attended her first nursing management meeting. She looked around the table at six serious faces, including Susan's, the director of nursing. Her peers immediately began to complain about staffing problems, especially sick call-offs. One nurse manager even accused some members of her unit of being lazy and undedicated. She looked to the DON (Director of Nursing) for support, but Susan just nodded and said nothing. The meeting left a sour taste in Chris' mouth.

To make her first week even more stressful, her night-shift charge RN called off sick. She contacted the usual part-time, fill-in registered nurses, but they all had prior commitments, at least the ones she could reach. Reticently, she asked Irene, the PM RN who replaced her as permanent charge nurse, to stay for a double shift. Irene looked like she was ready to cry, and shook her head no as she quickly explained her babysitter could not stay overnight. Therefore, Irene could not help out by covering this crucial position. Chris felt frustrated and alone.

Chris called the nursing office, asking if there were any other part-time RNs who might be available for a night shift. The nursing office secretary said she would consult with the PM nursing supervisor to try to fill this need, but sounded somewhat abrupt to Chris. Chris felt maybe the director would view her as less than competent because she could not fill the call off herself. She could feel not only sweat at the nape of her neck now, but also a knot in her stomach. Although the nursing office, with Marie's help, did come through for her and the night shift was covered, Chris felt she already might not be seen as an effective leader. It did not help that, the next day, Darlene made a sarcastic remark to her and rolled her eyes when Chris asked her to help look over the next month's dayshift schedule to try to ensure she gave that staff their usual days off, if possible. Chris thought this could be a way to engage Darlene as more of a colleague, but this attempt had obviously failed. She was beginning to feel more like a failure herself.

Chris began to feel more frustrated, alone, and disempowered. She did not feel comfortable turning to her new peer group, either, as the tone of the first nursing managers' meeting was negative and almost apathetic to her. She decided to let her staff know her expectations of them, although she was not sure exactly what she would say. Putting on an air of confidence on the outside, but feeling less sure of herself inwardly, Chris called a dayshift staff meeting and laid out her expectations in nearly a "laying down the law" way to her four full-time staff members. The results of that meeting were far from stellar.

She could feel the coldness of the new staff the next day. No one even greeted her. Chris knew she had made a big mistake. She felt miserable. Why had she taken on this role? Why had she come across so autocratically to her new staff? Suddenly she realized she was only alone because she had not asked for help. She did have a mentor, even though she worked another shift. Marie was the one person she could trust to be both honest and upfront with Chris, and at the same time, always help her find answers to tough problems.

Chris waited until the end of the day and called Marie after her day staff went home. Dejected, she told Marie what happened and what she did. Marie smiled, saying it was not unusual for new managers to try to assert their authority by coming across as dominant. Marie continued, sharing that asserting authority in this way actually often interfered with a person becoming an effective leader because then her staff wouldn't become willing team members.

CHAPTER ONE:

Remember, Listening is Key

Marie asked Chris what seemed to work for her on the evening shift, since she created a harmonious, effective team there. Chris answered that she would get her staff's concerns, she would invite their ideas when problem solving, and, in general, she would listen. Marie smiled and responded, "You followed the 80-20 rule." Chris asked what that meant, and Marie explained, "Listen 80 percent of the time, talk 20 percent." Chris thought back and realized she generally followed this rule consistently with her evening team.

Chris vowed she would try listening to the day staff starting the next morning. She walked with more genuine confidence unto her unit. She sat in an open posture, with her hands resting in her lap and, since she was wearing slacks, her legs slightly apart and only crossed at the ankles. She smiled warmly at her new staff and modestly stated that she felt she had gotten off on the wrong foot with her dayshift team. Then she asked each team member to share what they felt "worked" for this team and any concerns they had presently, including working with a new leader. Even Darlene looked surprised at this point. However, one by one, the team shared their accomplishments and strengths and some concerns.

She was sensitive both to what the staff said and how they said it. She watched facial expressions and body language as each team member spoke so she could try to decode any "real meaning" of what the person was saying. For example, when Darlene spoke, her pace was curt, her tone at times sounded impatient, her posture was rigidly straight, and her affect was tense.

Ida, an LPN, smiled a lot and nodded, then expounded on all the good points about the staff and how well they took care of patients. She seemed to watch for a reaction from Chris before continuing and even welcomed Chris to the team. She kept a smile on her face and talked somewhat rapidly. Chris was not sure whether Ida was sharing her true feelings or not, but thought it might be important to Ida that she was liked. After several minutes, however, Chris found it was necessary to gently help Ida summarize her ideas so other team members could have a chance to share.

Sarah was a soft-spoken CNA. She had no concerns about the staff, but tentatively asked Chris what changes she might want to make. She looked nervous when asking this question. Chris could feel Sarah might have some trouble dealing with changes.

Charles, another CNA, remained quiet during most of the meeting, nodded a lot, and looked seriously interested in everything each other team member said, taking notes along the way. He asked Chris a few detail-oriented questions. He, too, said everybody was "nice" to work with on the dayshift, and he did not have any concerns. His affect was fairly placid, and Chris found him hard to read.

Whenever Chris was unsure what one of her team was asking or saying, she requested clarification. For example, she gently asked Sarah what changes she anticipated Chris might make. Sarah, a little reluctantly, shared that she was not sure, but that it was a little scary for her when a new supervisor came, as there usually were changes made, sometimes fairly rapidly. Chris reassured Sarah that she would first assess the teamwork, etc. as it was, and only make changes if necessary. Sarah's affect seemed to soften and she looked less nervous in response.

Chris also knew that because she was rather intuitive, often she felt she just "knew" what other people were trying to communicate. Luckily she had been married for five years and her husband reminded her —more than once—that she was not a "mind reader." Therefore, Chris knew the value of clarifying what the other person meant by asking him or her. After all, the "eye of the beholder" sometimes was, well, dead wrong.

She was reminded of an old movie she saw in nursing school, where a woman rang her next door neighbor's doorbell, wanting to borrow a cup of sugar. When her neighbor opened the door, he was covered in red blotches and was holding a knife, also covered in red. Behind him she saw a woman, lying on her side facing away from the door, on a table, in a red dress. She was not moving. The woman screamed, thinking her neighbor had murdered the woman. Startled, the model sat up quickly and, as the "alleged" murderer moved slightly sideways, Chris could see the easel and paint pallet in the corner. What appeared to be a murder was only an artist painting a model who was wearing a red dress, and the knife he was holding was a pallet knife, covered in red paint. Chris thus learned appearances can be deceiving. So even though her meeting seemed to go fairly smoothly, she was aware she had a lot of work ahead of her to really get to know her new staff and get them to work as a team, with her as the leader.

Although no big changes were made—and of course there were issues raised that Chris could not address, at least not immediately— most of her staff, with the exception of Darlene, of course, nodded and smiled at her when she left the meeting. Really listening seemed to be a key to opening up communication. Chris understood that staying neutral also helped others to feel safe and share their concerns and feelings, which is the beginning of gaining trust and is a cornerstone of getting a team to follow a new leader.

What this new manager learned during her first few days was to open up communication by really listening. Sometimes, when a new person in authority feels unsure or even insecure in a position of greater authority, the natural tendency is to try to be or at least look strong as a way to assert oneself and gain the respect of the team. However, as you can see from Chris' experience, just the opposite usually occurs. Listening takes a lot of concentration and some energy. It also takes patience, because often when you ask people for their ideas or concerns, it may take quite some time for them to express themselves, at least authentically. Depending on many factors, some people may need more coaxing to talk, and others may need some gentle limits to "bottom line" their input.

Some of the tips Chris learned and could pass along to other new managers include:

1. Smile. It helps people feel more at ease.
2. Sit in an open posture with your hands relaxed in your lap, and both feet either comfortably on the floor or crossed at the ankles to show an openness that invites people to interact with

you. Be aware that if you often fold your arms or cross your legs at the knees, especially if you feel nervous, you present a closed posture which can be misinterpreted, signaling non-verbally that you are not interested in anything anyone else has to say. Be aware how your back is placed in your chair. Do you tend to slouch a bit? This posture often gives the impression that you feel insecure. On the other hand, do you sit stiffly erect? This posture says "stay away" to many people, or indicates a general rigidity. Sitting with an open posture, then, would include sitting fairly straight in your chair, but not stiffly erect.

3. Encourage each person to share, understanding there are different personality styles and some need coaxing to talk, while others need help to "bottom line" what they say.

4. Remember to let individuals finish their thoughts before responding. Sometimes in an effort to give some good feedback, it is easy to talk over quieter members.

5. Nod or show in some other way that you are understanding what staff members are saying, or say something like "uh huh" at times to let people know you continue to follow them. That does not necessarily mean you agree with everything they are saying, just that you are taking the time and effort to listen to their thoughts, ideas or concerns.

6. Be cognizant of the tone, speed, clarity, etc. of your speech. Some people talk rapidly when they feel nervous. Some tend to drop the end of sentences to a softer level or mumble when uncomfortable, making it hard for people to hear them when they speak.

In addition, although it takes more effort, try to become aware of how your overall tone comes across. Watch for non-verbal feedback from your staff. Some really savvy leaders often practice before a meeting, etc. using a mirror and a tape recorder to become more aware how they may come across to others as well.

7. A really hard thing for new managers to master is to admit they don't have to have all the answers or can't fix all the problems

presented. However, just knowing they are being heard often helps staff deal with a difficult situation, change etc.

8. Let your staff know you can't fix everything. Sometimes managers, especially nursing leaders, feel challenged when they really can't make a problem better. Being oriented as caretakers, it is sometimes the self expectation that we are "all things to all people all the time." While this is funny, I remember that I had dubbed this as the job description for an off-shift nursing supervisor in my early leadership days. Keep in mind that just being heard sometimes can dramatically reduce the stress level of a team, even before any action is taken to remedy issues that might be able to be modified or changed.

9. Listening is a powerful tool to help build a team. If members feel they are being heard by their leader, they often immediately feel more valued. It is one way to establish a leadership position because in order to be effective as a leader, the rest of the team has to accept that person's authority.

10. Although listening may seem like a passive way to deal with issues, this healthy type of listening is called *active listening,* Vidal (2008) because when you get really good at it, you receive the information through the use of at least two senses. You hear the words, and you see non-verbal communication which may or may not be concurrent with the words. It takes some work to function at this level of communication, especially when new at the job, but it can be fine tuned.

11. Although at first it may seem backwards because most new managers may feel they need to let people know who they are and what they expect, listening is the first key to building a highly effective, cohesive and harmonious team.

CHAPTER TWO

Expect Differences of Interpretation

Chris felt more confident after facilitating a meeting where concerns seemed to be shared openly. She also felt good about herself for focusing not just on concerns but on positives as well. However, Chris soon realized that not everyone interprets many issues, or even what seems to be surface conversation, in the same way.

Chris worked with a diverse group of people. Darlene, for example, was a strong, single, fifty year old, middle class Caucasian nurse who also had a BSN degree. Ida was a bubbly, talkative thirty-nine year old LPN, originally from a poor village in Mexico and a mother of four children. Charles was a sixty-nine year old African-American CNA, from a working class family. He worked for the hospital for over twenty years and seemed to have a close relationship with another mature man who worked in the dietary department. Sarah was the youngest member of the team, being only twenty years old. She was a CNA of Middle Eastern heritage and had aspirations of going to nursing school the next year. However, she was also "madly in love" with a young man who was overseas in the army and was not sure whether she also wanted to get married and have a "houseful of children".

Chris realized she was leading a really diverse team with a dramatic age difference. She asked Marie how some of these differences might impact her ability to effectively create a winning team. Chris shared that Charles was sixty-nine years old. Marie identified Charles as a "traditional" person, or "Traditionalist", Schneider (2010) i.e., a person born before 1945. She expounded that traditional people were usually very loyal, especially to an institution or facility, for years. Chris confirmed that Charles had a twenty year work history with a good track record. Marie cautioned, however, that traditionalists often experience the most stress dealing with progress. They seem to want to hold onto "the way things were always done." Chris asked, "Like the old saying, 'if it ain't broke, don't fix it'?" Marie smiled and nodded.

Chris identified Darlene as a fifty-year-old. Marie rolled her eyes, because Marie was in her late fifties herself. Marie commented that that made Darlene a baby boomer (born between 1945 and 1965). She continued that baby boomers tend to be hard working and are sometimes even considered to be workaholics. They tend to be strong willed, and somewhat independent. Chris nodded and half smiled as she affirmed, "You hit the nail on the head with Darlene." Chris then added she felt Darlene would be her biggest challenge and Marie smiled back knowingly.

When Chris shared that Ida was thirty-nine years old, Marie replied, "Oh, a Generation Xer! I bet she wants to balance her work life with her home/family life and she probably won't volunteer for any extra hours or projects." Chris looked pensive, because at times call-offs were an issue even on her harmonious evening shift, albeit rarely. She made a mental note to herself that Ida would likely be her last choice to ask to stay over for a double shift when it was necessary. Luckily, she had enough part-timers she could ask first, whom she planned to call in under Plan A should it be needed.

The last full-time member, Chris continued, was the youngest. Sarah was a sweet twenty year old girl, who wanted to be a nurse some day, or a wife and mother, or maybe both. Marie laughed, and said, "A Generation Y person. They are also called the 'what's in it for me?' generation. On a positive note they are people who want to have it all in life and tend to be lively. However, they also can be the most difficult to engage when the going gets really rough. They tend to move around a lot and have little loyalty to any one place or person." When Chris looked sad— she already had taken a liking to Sarah—Marie added, "Remember being a certain age is only one small aspect of a person, and there are no hard and fast rules that every person fits into a generational box just because they are a certain number of years old." Chris smiled then, feeling she just learned one more tool to help assess her team's strengths and weaknesses along with good ideas on how to more effectively engage each member.

Chris then identified another aspect of diversity in her new team. She shared there were several cultural differences, both in socioeconomic background and in ethnicity. She understood that these two issues could at times cause some conflicts, but that also sharing some specialness of each culture, such as sampling ethnic foods, and asking about holidays like *Cinco de Mayo* or possibly *Kwanza*, could be helpful in creating bonds as well. When she asked for Marie's opinion on how she should approach cultural diversity, Marie smiled proudly, and complimented Chris on her observations.

Then Marie quoted new studies that stress looking for commonalities—what is "just like me"—to start. She said the studies showed most people in a common workplace wanted to feel they were respected, included in decision making, etc., and that their ethnicity, sex, religion, or lifestyle choice did not matter. Often it was better, she added, to let the other people share what they felt comfortable with about any specific cultural tradition or religious belief, or whether or not they wished to discuss their lifestyle choice. Allowing people their privacy about personal issues while showing interest if they want to share, shows respect for staff members as individuals. Chris nodded, and felt her mentor had given her another great insight: "look for the similarities to build a team, while respecting the differences."

Marie asked, "Chris, are you ready for a challenge for your next team meeting?" Chris eagerly agreed. "Another key to help understand diverse individuals and better communicate your messages clearly is to understand that people tend to communicate in a preferred mode," Marie began. She then introduced the four modes: visual, auditory, kinesthetic and cerebral/thinker. Marie shared that she had read a classic book, *Influencing with Integrity*, for the first time when it was new in 1984 (Laborde). It was based on the work of Dr. Milton Erickson, who had been bedridden for a few years with a long illness. He learned to watch and listen intently to his caretakers and, instead of feeling sorry for himself, actually did experiential research. Out of his work came neuro-linguistic programming (or NLP), which was the basis for this creative work that Marie found to be a beneficial way to help a leader understand clearly what each team member was trying to communicate and even help "translate" messages when needed.

As a leader, slowing down and actually noting your own thought patterns can help you to better understand yourself and the world around you. Marie emphasized that we all structure the world we live in differently.

Marie continued that this book had helped her assess people's primary modes of communication by watching their eye movements as they spoke as well as listening to their tone of voice and what descriptive words they tended to use. Eye movements showed which representational system a person might be using at that time, emphasizing that while most people use one preferred mode, they also usually utilize at least one other fairly often. These movements indicate whether a person is making pictures, listening to some internal tape/dialogue, or concentrating on feelings.

Marie explained that visually oriented people tend to look up to the left or right. However, they sometimes also just appear to defocus and look straight ahead, usually concentrating on something about two feet in front of their face, while they make pictures of what they are saying. Auditorily oriented people may keep their eyes level but move them to the right or left. Alternatively, they may look down and to the left. Kinesthetic or feeling oriented people tend to look down and to the right.

Marie continued that visuals use words such as *see*, *clear* or *colorful*; i.e., visual words. They use expressions such as *I see what you mean* and *I get the picture*. Since they tend to breathe high in the chest, they may sound a bit breathless and their voices may sound high-pitched. They speak more rapidly than other people. They also tend to tense their neck and shoulders as they tighten up to make their mind pictures clearer.

Auditory people tend to have melodious voices. They are often musicians or radio announcers and in terms of numbers there are fewer of them than the other styles. They also tend to talk to themselves (not out loud) in dialogue. Because they tend to have deep discussions with themselves about issues, they sometimes also have trouble making decisions. They breathe in the middle of the chest; their tone is lower and their talking pace is somewhat slower than visuals. They have a more rhythmic tempo in their speech, not jerky as visuals can be or leaving blank spaces as kinesthetics often do. Thus, listening to an auditory speak is usually a pleasant experience. They will use phrases, Marie shared, such as *that rings a bell* and *I hear you*. To relax or deal with any discord in life, they tend to listen to CDs or go out and enjoy a symphony.

Kinesthetics breathe in the lower abdomen, and their voices tend to be lower than the first two. They leave spaces when they talk so they can check in with their feelings intermittently.

They use phrases such as *need to get in touch with what is going on, get a feel for the problem, remove the stumbling block* or *untangle the knot.* They tend to either like or hate. They feel *warm, cold* or *lukewarm* about almost everything.

Cerebrals/thinkers don't respond to raw emotions, but rather to labels they give to perceptions. In other words they filter what they experience through their minds, and try to describe the experience rather than experience it. It is hard to detect this style because they often use the same eye movements as other styles, so a better way is to watch for an overall cautious look as the thinker searches for a "perfect" description. They will use words such as *I think*.

A key both to communicating more clearly with each of these representational styles and to helping each member of your team who uses a different style to feel heard and respected, is to try to match the other person's tone, pace and words. Making this extra effort helps to gain what NLP people call *rapport,* Laborde (1984)with them. However, Marie added, to make life a little more complicated, people tend to move from one mode to another. It makes a difference for many people whether they are interacting with good friends and family, or with colleagues and supervisors at work, for example.

In order to make the basic translation from one mode to another more clear, here are some examples from *Influencing with Integrity,*Laborde, (1984 p.71):

Visual: "My future looks hazy"
Match: "When I look to the future, it is not clear."
Translates to:
Auditory: "I can't tune into my future."
Kinesthetic: "I can't get a feel for what's going to happen."

Auditory: "Sarah doesn't listen to me."
Match: "Sarah goes deaf when I talk."
Translate:
Visual: "Sarah never sees me, even when I am present."
Kinesthetic: "Sarah doesn't know I'm alive."

> Kinesthetic: "Mary gets churned up on Mondays, when the report
> is due."
> Match: "Mary gets agitated and nervous on Mondays."
> Translate:
> Visual: "Mary can't focus on Mondays when the report is due."
> Auditory: "Mary hears lots of static on Mondays when the report
> is due."

"Oh, I think I get it!" Chris said. "Hey, Marie, does that make me a thinker?" Marie just smiled again. "I am glad you are taking on this challenge, Grasshopper; let me know how your next meeting goes and what you have learned."

Chris planned to be observant at a deeper level. She would keep in mind the possible age and cultural diversity differences, but focus on not just what a team member would say, but how the person said it. Chris also knew her special challenge would probably be Darlene, not just because she was a hard working baby boomer with twenty more years of experience than Chris, but because Darlene may express frustration in any manner of ways, due to feeling slighted in not getting the nurse manager position.

To recap: Chris learned some valuable lessons to start building her new team, with herself as their leader:

1. Be aware that each generation tends to have certain work ethics and values. Trying to get all the members of a team to believe the same way about work can cause a lot of frustration for the leader.

2. Most workplaces nowadays are culturally diverse. However, looking for what people have in common often helps build cohesive teams more rapidly.

3. Respecting people's ethnicity and religious and sexual preferences is important, but equally important is respecting their right to privacy. If people feel it's safe/comfortable to share some of their culture's specialness, they will do so in due time.

4. To understand that we only *think* we all speak the same language is a key to avoid misunderstandings. By being flexible and being able to translate someone else's representational

mode, a leader also helps the other person feel understood and recognized.

5. Overall, Chris learned to be observant on many different levels, assessing both her team and the issues she might need to address to help establish herself as the new leader.

Let's eavesdrop on Chris' next meeting. Chris began by asking how the week was going, keeping to neutral language to start. Ida beamed and excitedly shared with them that her oldest daughter had won a shiny gold medal at school for her artwork, which made her mother very happy. She had purchased a beautiful new pink dress for church that her husband said made her look ten pounds thinner and she was starting a beginners class in oil painting. Ida added that her daughter was her inspiration and she now believed that she too could become an artist, an aspiration she had had as a child. Her voice was high pitched as she shared her story in quick spurts. She looked up to the right or left often as if to access pictures of what she was saying. Chris gently brought the subject back to patient care, but complimented Ida with, "I see you had a really colorful week," to which Ida smiled. Chris then asked more specifically what positive or challenging patient centered issues were occurring that the staff could discuss as a team.

Darlene looked sourly at Chris and sighed. Sarah timidly mentioned she was worried about Mrs. G., as Mrs G. had told her that her family had not called for days. Sarah couldn't imagine anyone failing to call and talk to such an interesting and nice lady. Chris replied that it seemed Mrs. G felt her needs were not being heard by her family, to which Sarah nodded.

Chris noted Sarah kept her gaze at eye level but looked to her left when she spoke, and her voice was melodious.

Chris then asked Sarah how she might help Mrs. G. take the initiative to call at least one member of her family so she could hear a loving voice. Sarah committed to helping Mrs. G. choose the family member that she would most like to talk with and help her actually make the phone call. Sarah smiled..

Charles looked as if he wanted to say something, but remained pensive instead. Chris turned to him and asked what he thought was going right this week, and if anything else might need to be discussed. Charles looked pensive again. In an almost flat tone, he shared that he thought one of his patients may be declining, because he was unable to work his crossword that morning from the paper. Chris thanked Charles for sharing this important information, and replied she would personally check Mr. B. for a mental status exam in case there was a chance he had experienced another small stroke.

Chris looked at Darlene, who returned a warning glance that seemed to say, "Don't ask me, I obviously don't feel like sharing anything with you." Chris acknowledged the look with just a nod and an attempted friendly smile. Overall, Chris felt pretty good about this meeting, but knew she would need to talk over her main concern—Darlene—that evening with Marie.

Chris felt she had been able to match her new day staff's representational modes—well most of them. She felt she would at least need to begin to address Darlene's behavior because she realized Darlene's negative non-verbal communication in meetings could undermine her attempts to build a new, harmonious team. However, Chris was not sure exactly how to approach this sensitive issue. Darlene seemed to have been a valuable member of the day shift for at least the three years Chris worked on the evening shift, and when they were colleagues they had a mutually respectful, although not overly close, relationship. While Chris could feel her neck muscles tighten when Darlene walked into a room, she also instinctively knew she had to do something about her reaction to Darlene's presence as well, if she wanted to create an authentic team.

Chris was relieved to see Marie's smiling face that evening. She began by sharing some of her observations about each of her staff's representational modes. Chris pictured Ida as probably being a visual person because of the colorful language she used, her rapid high-pitched speech pattern and upward eye movements. She heard Sarah's mid-range voice and auditory language clearly and noted her level back and forth eye movements. She identified Charles' ability to express his concern by sharing facts about his patient's change in behavior, along with his at times almost poker face and near monotone voice, as traits of a thinker.

Marie, noticing how Chris was using language from three of the four representational modes accurately as she described most of her full-time staff, just smiled proudly. However, Marie could tell Chris was not entirely happy with the outcome of her meeting. Marie commented that Chris had said nothing about Darlene's chosen mode. She paused a few seconds in order to let Chris continue. Chris did. She expressed her frustration with Darlene's sighing and rolling her eyes as Chris began the meeting. While it seemed the meeting had gone well overall, she continued, it was surprising how just this one person could seem to spoil everything. "Everything?" Marie asked. Chris then was able to laugh at herself a bit. After all, Darlene was not really that powerful. She could not really ruin everything, only affect the tone of the room and, if Chris allowed it, make her feel uncomfortable and off center.

Chris shared these thoughts and feelings with Marie, who then asked, "So what representational mode do you think Darlene uses most?" Chris was somewhat taken aback, expecting Marie to be sympathetic to her feelings of self doubt. She thought for a few seconds, then realized Darlene was probably using a feeling mode. She sighed, recalling that when Darlene spoke her voice was usually low-pitched and strong sounding. Even though Darlene rolled her eyes during the meeting, Chris recognized that she usually looked somewhat downward when she spoke.

Chris realized she needed to meet Darlene with feeling language. Her own, more thinker language might not be the best fit for Darlene. She shared these observations with Marie. Marie agreed that using more feeling oriented language with Darlene might help engage her. She also encouraged Chris to talk with Darlene on a one-to-one basis before trying to do so in a group. When Chris asked why, Marie explained that people who are having trouble accepting a new leader, especially one like Darlene who was older than the new leader, had been on the day shift first and who might interact on a more feeling level, often need an audience in order to express their dissatisfaction. On their own, they may be more easily engaged.

Chris asked Marie what she thought was the best way to actually approach Darlene. Marie shared an old Indian saying, "Walk a mile in her moccasins." Chris was not sure exactly what that meant so she asked Marie to clarify. Marie asked Chris to imagine the tables were turned. What would she think and how would she feel if a younger nurse from another shift took the job she felt she deserved? Chris hesitated a minute. Then she said she got the point. She vowed to talk with Darlene the next day. Her goal was to at least begin the process of engaging Darlene in a healthy conversation.

Chris asked Darlene to come to the nurse's lounge for a few minutes when she was sure no one else was there. She could have asked Darlene into her office but thought better of it. After all, being asked into the boss's office might come across like a student being called into the principal's office. She did not want to put Darlene on the defensive. Darlene followed Chris into the lounge with a pouting face. Chris asked Darlene to have a cup of coffee with her. Darlene looked puzzled, as if she was unsure what was happening. Chris candidly stated, "Darlene, you are a very experienced nurse and I want you to know how valued you are as a member of this unit's team." Darlene blinked, as if in shock. The pout on her face softened. She looked directly at Chris and mumbled, "Thank you". Chris continued, "I wanted you to know that I understand it might be hard to have a younger nurse from the evening shift become the nurse manager. I know you wanted the job, and frankly I don't know why the director of nursing chose me. I am sorry if you felt disappointed. However, I really need your support to help make this a harmonious team again. Will you help me?" Darlene looked stunned. She seemed to be speechless. Then she blurted out, "I felt rotten when they announced you would be coming as my boss, I admit it. It felt unfair, even though I always kind of liked you as a person, that you should get the job over me. I guess I was being rude to you, though, when I sighed and rolled my eyes in the meeting." Chris smiled at Darlene's self awareness. She took the high road by asking Darlene to join her in starting over. Darlene mumbled that she would try.

Chris felt hopeful after this meeting with Darlene. She thought it could be the start of a more cohesive and less stressful relationship. However, Chris was also realistic enough to know this one small step was probably not a major breakthrough, just a beginning. With a hopeful tone she shared what had happened with Marie, but also told her she was only cautiously optimistic about the current situation with Darlene. Then she discussed the possibility of engaging Darlene further as her right hand person. She admitted to Marie that she was not sure if that was the most beneficial way to engage her present nemesis, as she was aware the downside might be that Darlene would be perceived as having too much power by the other staff. Marie did not give Chris a definitive yes or no to this dilemma. Instead, she asked Chris to think about it for awhile as she was still in the assessment phase of her new leadership role.

Chris then exclaimed enthusiastically, "I just had an *aha* moment!" Marie looked inquisitively at Chris, but waited for her to continue. "I am using the nursing process: Sharma (2004) assessment (including diagnosis of problems), planning, implementation and evaluation, or I guess we could abbreviate it as making A PIE." Marie and Chris both laughed at this pun. Marie then beamed at Chris proudly and said, "Another great insight, Grasshopper." Chris smiled, as she loved the re-runs of the show about a Chinese monk who learned at the feet of a master teacher both martial arts and life lessons. The older monk referred fondly to the younger as "Grasshopper." Chris liked this reference as she believed Marie was in some ways her teacher and in others her mentor.

Right now, Chris thought, she needed to spend some time further assessing her team and their needs and concerns before actually intervening to try to change any behaviors. She shared with Marie that she would not confront Darlene's behavior unless it became overtly hostile. Marie asked Chris what *hostile* meant. Chris stated that "yelling, throwing something—especially if it is thrown at someone—or threatening to hurt someone was definitely not going to be tolerated. I would have to immediately intervene if any of those behaviors occurred." Marie nodded and clarified, "In other words, any aggressive behavior that either would or potentially could harm someone else on the team emotionally or physically will not be tolerated." Chris agreed that those were good parameters, and that Darlene had not crossed the line into "hostile" behavior. Chris went on to say that she wanted the passive aggressive non-verbal behavior to cease soon as well, as it tended to break her concentration, and negatively affect her confidence.

Marie then asked Chris how she could keep her concentration and self confidence high while slowly trying to diminish Darlene's difficult behaviors. Chris thought for a moment, then commented that she had done breathing exercises and positive affirmations in the past. Marie asked which ones seemed to help most and Chris said that taking three deep breaths while saying "I am centered" seemed to help—when she remembered to use these techniques. Marie then asked how Chris could cue herself to use these techniques. Chris responded she was not sure, but then thought another moment and exclaimed, "Oh, I could utilize Darlene's behavior as my cue. Whenever she sighs and rolls her eyes I could say to myself, 'there's my cue,' and start deep breathing and saying my affirmation." Marie again looked pleased. "So you can start by turning a behavior that formerly elicited a negative response from you into a cue that you need to utilize the new response consciously," Chris agreed that having a positive coping strategy ready would curb an automatic negative reaction to Darlene's sighs and rolling eyes.

Chris vowed to utilize the new response strategy the next time she encountered Darlene's passive-aggressive behavior. When she saw Darlene the next morning, however, something seemed different. Darlene actually half smiled at Chris. This was a surprise, albeit a pleasant one. Darlene's voice, while still low, seemed less strong sounding, as well. Chris asked Darlene her opinion after a report about a potential downward change in one patient's condition and Darlene responded with a good, solid treatment plan adjustment. Chris complimented Darlene and asked her to implement the change. Although Chris did not overtly ask Darlene to become her second in command, she did open the door for Darlene to come through and begin to work more as a team member whose ideas and input were important enough to be recognized and implemented. Chris, who also at times and with some effort could get in touch with her own body's messages, was aware that her neck muscles were more relaxed and she didn't have any sweat at the back of her neck.

Chris then made her daily rounds throughout the unit. She talked to each patient briefly, letting the new patients know who she was, and asking them how they were doing, etc. She also checked in with each staff member to see how each was doing. In turn, each greeted her, and their affects showed they appreciated the interest shown in this informal way. Of course, Ida had to relate all about the beautiful dinner she made last night, and how pretty her daughter looked getting ready for her first dance, giving great detail about the color and style of the girls' dress, shoes and purse. Chris knew this was Ida's way of bonding, so even though she was more of a bottom line person herself, she listened intently to Ida's story for a few minutes. When an advantageous moment arose—a patient's room buzzer went off—Chris graciously excused herself to continue her rounds. Chris was somewhat upset with herself that she felt a bit irritated with Ida for taking up her time with meaningless chatter, but remembered Ida was a visual person and they tended to give a detailed description of just about anything they shared. Chris just put that note in the back of her head, and gently reminded herself that each of her staff was a unique individual with different needs. She also gently let herself off the hook. After all, she too was an individual with her own needs and uniqueness.

At this point Chris was beginning to understand that leading a group of diverse people would be challenging. The evening shift she had just left was more homogenous. All the staff were about the same age, although culturally diverse, with the exception of one older LPN, who in some ways had actually mentored Chris when she first came to the shift as permanent charge nurse. However, Chris never felt threatened in any way by Clara. Chris thought long and hard about why Clara, who was an LPN and at times seemed to know more about patient care than Chris, never made Chris feel uncomfortable or emotionally threatened. It hit Chris that Clara had a quiet way of gently letting Chris know the ropes without coming across as bossy or either overtly or covertly hostile. She just plain knew a lot and Chris respected people from whom she could learn something. Clara was a fountain of practical knowledge, and her bedside manner was so kind, loving and positive; the patients seemed to brighten up when she came into a room. Chris also remembered that when Clara was passing medications, it even seemed as though patients did not use their nurse call bells as much. Her calm, gentle but caring attitude just seemed to be contagious.

At that moment Chris wished she could trade Darlene for that supportive colleague, because even though Ida might be a bit irritating to Chris, Darlene surely was the one team member that Chris identified as being the most difficult to truly engage, despite the brief inroad they recently made together. Chris then got another idea of how to engage Darlene. She would try to identify something Darlene did really well, and point out this asset to her. Of course, it was somewhat difficult for Chris to think of anything she could observe the day charge nurse doing that would fit that bill. It hit her then that maybe the next step to engaging Darlene was to just observe her at work without being too obvious. After all, Darlene had been in nursing a good many years and must have some strengths, skills or other positive attributes that Chris could praise.

Chris became more enthusiastic after deciding to look for Darlene's attributes. She was almost impatient for the day shift to end so she could share this idea with Marie. Marie again just smiled enigmatically at Chris after hearing this new insight. She replied, "Yes, look for the good, and you likely will help create more of it." The nurse manager thought this was a wise way to act.

The next day Chris came to the unit with a renewed positive attitude. Today she would just concentrate on finding the good in Darlene. After report she noticed Darlene talking with Charles about one of the most ill patients on the unit. Darlene went with Charles to help him transfer this very debilitated larger person into a wheelchair. She even let the patient know she was a nurse and patted the older lady's hand while she engaged the patient to try to help as much as she could. Darlene also reassured the patient that she and Charles would make sure she was safe while she transferred, as that particular person previously told Chris she was really afraid of falling and breaking a hip or some other bone. Chris could see the patient's face clearly. The older woman seemed determined to get up from her bed, but looked for non-verbal reassurance from both Darlene and Charles. Interesting, thought Chris, Mrs. P. looked first for reassurance from Darlene. That was one positive Chris would share with Darlene. However, she knew it would be important how she shared this observation, so she would not come across to a strong personality like Darlene as being condescending. She also had to be sure she was being genuine so her compliment would not be misinterpreted as being manipulative, but rather as an expression of appreciation of Darlene's special contribution from her supervisor.

Chris decided to just put the emphasis on how Mrs. P. reacted to Darlene's reassurance and how Darlene took the initiative to help transfer the patient rather than waiting for the other CNA to finish helping another patient. She looked Darlene in the eye and shared her appreciation. Darlene again looked at Chris as if she was not sure what to think. She hurriedly said, "Thank you for noticing," and briskly went to her next duty. Chris was not sure exactly how well this interaction had gone, but thought she would continue to look for more good in Darlene.

A funny thing happened to Chris in that moment. She began to feel differently about Darlene. She remembered reading a book about something she thought was called the "law of attraction." Anyway, she remembered it taught that you should concentrate on what you want, not what you don't want. Chris wanted a harmonious, effective team. She did not want a nemesis. She began to experience a shift in her thinking. She vowed to keep her thoughts and goals positive, while trying to engage a person who seemed not even to like her. Somehow she did not feel so nervous or uncomfortable around Darlene the rest of the day. Instead, Chris made a conscious effort to see all the good things Darlene did. She did not share any more of them that day, as her intuition told her that, even though she was beginning to see Darlene in a more positive way, it might take Darlene a longer time to really believe that Chris really meant what she said about valuing Darlene.

Chris realized other people may view the world differently than she did. Chris came from a stable two-parent family. Her older brother was somewhat protective, as well as a tease sometimes, but she always felt safe with him. Her older sister at times could be a bit bossy, but was also always helpful, especially with their mother after dad died. Her younger sister was a bit spoiled, being a "change of life baby," but she grew up to marry a loving man, and was raising two lovely daughters. Chris did not have children of her own—yet. However, she couldn't ask for a more supportive husband. He encouraged her to succeed in school, and when Chris expressed doubts about whether she was ready for this new position, he listened, but also pointed out her many qualities that he felt would make her a great leader. He had a way of helping Chris believe in herself, even when she felt unsure.

Her parents did not fight, drink or cheat on one another. What they said, they meant. If they disagreed about something, and of course they did at times, they usually just talked things out. Dad once in a while got quiet for a day or two, after he and her mother had a serious disagreement, but Chris learned later that was just a man "going into his cave" to work things out in his head. However, soon he would return to joking and holding mom's hand when they walked together. That memory always made Chris smile. She wondered how Darlene's family treated her and each other while she was growing up. Did her parents say what they meant and mean what they said? Or, did they say one thing and do another, or live by "do as I say, but not as I do," or some other way of living where the members could not trust each other. Just pondering how someone's family of origin could influence that person later on in life seemed to make the task of getting through to Darlene more daunting. Chris realized that even if she were able to recognize Darlene's attributes and give her a compliment, Darlene might not believe a word she spoke.

Chris again went to her mentor, Marie, to share this new insight. Marie looked serious. She suggested that Chris was dealing at a very deep level with what affects a team's ability to bond and become effective as a unit. Building trust was fundamental, but sometimes it took time. She continued that she did not know Darlene's family history, but that how a person was raised can definitely influence them the rest of their lives. People develop their ideas and beliefs about the world, themselves and other people at a young age. Attachment theory goes into detail about secure, insecure or chaotic relationships between a child and parent. "From knowing you, I can guess you probably came from a warm, loving and secure background," Marie said. Chris smiled.

When she thought about family holidays, the first memories were usually her older brother telling jokes just like dad used to, her older sister unveiling another especially delectable specialty dish, or her younger sister sharing her daughter's accomplishments. It made her smile just to think about her family. Of course no one was perfect, Chris knew that. However, while she herself loved planning to go home for the holidays, other peers had shared with her at different times in her career their dread of going home to be with their families. Chris was not sure how she, as Darlene's supervisor, could undo any damage that might have been done to Darlene as a child, especially if the situation were more serious than just a personality difference with Darlene feeling she had been passed over. She also did not know if her role of nurse manager was supposed to include even trying to repair a trust/bonding issue.

Chris decided, after talking it over with Marie, that while she would continue to try to look for the good in Darlene, she could only deal with this problem by showing Darlene consistency, being honestly appreciative of her, and also setting some healthy boundaries regarding behavioral issues if needed. She knew she was not a therapist, however, and there were limits to what she could do if Darlene did come from an insecurely attached family background. It saddened Chris to think that many people probably have been raised in such circumstances, like one nurse she recalled from her early days.

She had started the job at the same time as the other nurse. They were both working on continuing their nursing education to BSN level. Chris got promoted to a higher level staff nurse, while her friend was not promoted. Suddenly the person became hostile and even tried changing the primary care plan of one of Chris's patients without consulting with Chris. When confronted on this issue, the person began talking badly about Chris behind her back and giving Chris dirty looks. It made Chris so uncomfortable she felt on pins and needles every time she had to work with the other nurse. When that former friend finally left the unit, she admitted to Chris that she was mean to her because she felt that Chris was being nice solely out of political ambition. Chris was confounded until she remembered that nurse's father was a politician. Suddenly the ex-friend's behavior made perfect sense.

Chris realized she would need to choose where to set her boundaries while still trying to understand the reasons for Darlene's actions. Setting parameters would not be easy for Chris, as she admitted to herself that while she usually made decisions based rationally, she was also aware she had some trouble dealing with conflict. It hit Chris that a good deal of her team assessment applied to herself, as well. Chris always preferred working with people who were respectful, and ideally those who even seemed to like her.

She closed her eyes and recalled Darlene's face during her last meeting. She could feel her neck muscles tensing and was aware that her facial muscles were tightening up. Chris was amazed how much even imagining Darlene's face affected her own feeling of well being. She could also almost hear Darlene's loud sigh and could envision the day charge nurse rolling her eyes at the same time. Chris knew it would take some work on her part to learn not to react emotionally when someone like Darlene pushed her buttons. She concluded, however, that if she could remain calm, focused and centered—even when others were having trouble regulating their own emotions—she could also act as a role model. On the other hand, she became acutely aware that if she, as the designated leader, let others' behavior push her off center, how could she expect the rest of the team to stay focused and centered? If she wanted an effective and harmonious team, a priority would be for her to become mindful of her own reactions and try to modify any responses that seemed to be less than supportive to team cohesiveness.

Chris had been told once in the past that when she tried to set a limit on a nurse's unacceptable behavior while also feeling upset with that person, she came across in a condescending manner. She then knew that, before setting limits on any of Darlene's behavior she might deem unacceptable, Chris needed to emotionally remove herself somewhat from the situation. She was not sure exactly how to work on staying more emotionally distanced, however, while still coming across as a genuine human being.

When Marie came on shift, Chris shared her latest insight with her mentor. Marie agreed that self-assessment was an important skill to learn. She suggested Chris just continue to be aware of what behaviors were triggers for her. Marie reassured her that all people experience challenges to their self esteem. She explained that, contrary to popular belief, self esteem is dynamic and constantly developing, not just something that was totally developed in childhood.

She asked Chris to think of the five people she spent the most time with outside of work. Chris identified them as her husband, her two sisters, one brother and her closest friend. Marie then asked how she felt when she was with these people, and Chris immediately responded that she felt safe, valued and loved. She added she trusted these people with her innermost thoughts, feelings and life goals. They in turn were supportive of her, but were also honest if they disagreed with her, to her face. She went on to say that she never felt as if they would turn on her, talk badly about her behind her back, or put her down. Her face lit up when talking about these five support people. Marie smiled, and told Chris she had a very special family and best friend, which was great outside of work, to help Chris continue to grow as a person and recover from any self esteem assaults she might feel she experienced at work. Chris wished Marie had some more tangible advice about how to develop a healthy team interaction at work, where she could both give and receive positive support. However Chris, somewhat sadly, came to the realization that supportive and healthy family members/ friends were not always the type of people who surround many people.

What did Chris learn about leading a diverse team?

1. People have varying ways of interpreting the world around them.
2. Basically, when a new leader thinks about (feels, sees or hears) what staff members are trying to communicate, he or she may think about (feel, see or hear) the communication differently enough to misinterpret the messages and or behavior.
3. People communicate in four different modes—visual, auditory, kinesthetic (feeling) or thinker representational modes. They use language that represents their primary and/or secondary modes. They also exhibit different speech patterns, including rate and tone variations. Their eye movements tend to match their language. Thinkers are somewhat harder to read as their

affect may be subtle and their eye movements may vary, so listening to their chosen wording is most telling.

4. Age differences can also make an impact on the team. Traditionalists, baby boomers, Generation X and Generation Y people all share workplaces today. The specific work ethics are different. Traditionalits tend to be loyal to organizations for years, Baby boomers tend to be workaholic high achievers, Generation Xers want more balance in their work/home lives, and Generation Yers are the "what's in it for me?" folks. Each group has specific needs and fears. Therefore, motivating them to be most effective individually and as a team can be challenging.

5. While cultural diversity exists in the workplace, many modern studies show that looking for similarities and making sure people feel valued and included in the decision making process seem to be most important to diverse groups and a key way to help build a cohesive team.

6. Use of the nursing process, Sharma (2004)—assessment (including diagnosis of problems), planning, implementation and evaluation, —also helps a new leader to avoid jumping the gun; i.e., she or he should first assess what is working and what might be an issue or challenge before making any changes.

7. The most challenging part of the assessment process is self assessment. The new leader may want to ask herself (himself) the following vital questions: *What communication mode do I use most? To what generation do I belong? What is my basic personality style? Do I have any cultural biases?* Once a thorough assessment is completed, utilizing a combination of the above tools, ideally a leader will want to take her time making any changes. Planning first often helps alleviate much of the stress associated with change. However, sometimes changes may need to be implemented somewhat rapidly, because they may come from "above," i.e., upper management. In the next chapter we will follow Chris as she was faced with this challenge, and the need to continue the assessment process even after a fast change was implemented.

CHAPTER THREE:

Suspect Trouble when Changes Seem Too Smooth

Chris left the weekly nursing managers' meeting in shock. She had been told there no longer was a budget for a unit secretary. Although her unit only had one cross-shift person, working from 11:00 a.m. to 7:30 p.m.—the busiest times for admissions, discharges and visitors coming onto the unit—Chris knew this person's various duties would have to be absorbed by the nursing staff. Her unit tended to be a busy one, with an average of five admissions and discharges every day. Many of her patients also had caring families who visited regularly and sent flowers, etc. that had to be checked at the desk before being delivered. She feared this staffing cut would have a negative impact both on staff morale and patient care. Chris did not want to be the bearer of such bad news, especially because she recently reassured at least one of her staff that she did not plan to make any changes right away.

Chris had to give the team the bad news that day, according to the director of nursing, so she did not have any time to discuss how to approach this sensitive topic with Marie. She felt the sweat again on the back of her neck. This would not be an easy emergency meeting. Most difficult however, was that Chris had to tell Nell her job was cut, and she knew she had to give this news in a way that supported her boss as well as Nell. The director said they would pay the unit secretaries the rest of the week's salary, and since it was only Monday, this was at least one positive Chris could share. But she also had to tell Nell that this was her last shift. Chris

29

did not feel good about the decision, nor her role in communicating the bad news to both the unit secretary and the rest of the staff.

She decided to get a cup of coffee and do some relaxation breathing for a few minutes before she attempted to follow through with what she knew she had to do. She also spent a few minutes going over what she would say, and practiced (in the bathroom) saying it while watching her facial affect. She did not want to let on that she was disappointed and not in agreement with the loss of a role she felt was vital to good patient care, but knew it was her job to carry out the mission she was given by her supervisor.

Chris first took Nell aside, to the staff lounge. She got Nell a cup of coffee and began with sincerity, thanking her for her dedicated work and the positive influence she had both on patients and on the other staff. Luckily, although they worked in a fairly large medical center, the informal communication network had already alerted Nell of a possible layoff. She smiled sadly at Chris, and said, "It's all right honey, we have been expecting this news for awhile. You know I am a great-grandmother, and was thinking about retiring soon anyway. I will surely miss everybody, since I have been here almost as long as the unit, but I don't blame you." Chris felt tears starting to well up in her eyes, so she quickly got up, pretending she needed to get some cream for her coffee, to compose herself. She then reassured Nell she would give her excellent references if she wanted to work part-time anywhere else, and would love to hear from her to make sure she was doing okay. Nell shook Chris' hand, and returned to her work station to complete her tasks, as she always did, before she cleared out her personal things from her desk drawer.

Chris was daunted by the next step. She had to call together the staff, both her new team and her old evening shift team, to tell them the news. She decided to keep it brief during report time, to get the entire staff together. This would be her first test dealing with a management decision that was not in her control, but that she needed to both enforce and endorse, and it didn't feel very good.

When the staff came together at report time, Chris simply told them there was some news she needed to share with them. She matter-of-factly reported there was a need for a budget cut, and that cut would be the position of unit secretary. Those duties would need to be absorbed by the rest of the staff. She then invited the staff to think of ways to share covering the desk, etc. without impinging too much on patient care. The room was silent at first. Darlene then snarled, "Oh great, and how are we supposed to do decent patient care and cover the desk at the same time?" Chris did not have a quick answer to this one. The rest of the staff just looked first at Darlene, then at Chris. Chris took a deep breath, and said in a serious tone, "I know this will be a challenging adjustment for everyone. However, if each of us pitches in when charting or doing other desk-bound duties, we should be able to keep the front desk covered."

Darlene just huffed. Chris knew the unit secretary also created and stamped up new charts, broke down discharge chart paperwork, made out lab requisitions, and performed other support roles. Replacing her, even if all the staff worked together, would be stressful. However, Chris felt only Darlene seemed to be having trouble dealing with this change. The rest of the staff appeared more accepting of taking on the added work load. Even though Chris did not get any real feedback from the rest of her staff, she was at least briefly lulled into believing she would only need to engage Darlene to accept this change.

The next day, Chris came back onto the unit after report. She asked Darlene whether she had assigned anyone to cover the desk at different times. Darlene answered, "Oh, was I supposed to?" Chris knew this was probably Darlene's way of passive-aggressively acting out her feelings about the change.

Luckily, Chris was able to confer with Marie before deciding what she would do. Marie began, not by addressing Darlene's behavior, but instead by stating, "Chris, you are learning another important lesson. Suspect trouble when changes seem to go too smoothly." Chris pondered this pearl of wisdom for a minute. Maybe it was only Darlene who was being open with her reactions to this tough budget cut decision. Maybe the rest of the staff were still in shock or something. It reminded Chris of the five stages of grief she had studied in school. The first stage was shock and disbelief. Anger also was one of the stages, and she was aware that people often moved back and forth between the stages when they dealt with a loss. This key position surely was a significant loss to the team. It also occurred at an inopportune time, since Chris had not even had time to establish herself in her leadership position before she was forced to be the bearer of this bad news.

Chris shared her observations with Marie, who smiled back, and complimented Chris on being able to identify the complexity of this situation. If Chris only focused on the small picture, i.e., Darlene acting in a passive-aggressive manner, she would likely respond in a way that might make the situation worse. It could be that Darlene, being older and used to more abrupt changes in the work place than her peers, was the only person who may have jumped ahead to the anger stage of grief.

Chris discussed this possibility with Marie, who gave her an encouraging "uh huh" and a nod. Marie then asked Chris what her own feelings were about the loss of Nell and Nell's position.

Chris was open, sharing how she thought there could be other ways to cut the budget so that neither her staff nor patients had to suffer. She admitted to feeling awful having to be the one to let a really good employee go, which made her feel almost as if she had fired Nell. Chris said she felt a knot tighten in her stomach when she asked Nell to join her for a cup of coffee. She thought that at least she had created a somewhat supportive place and way to tell Nell. She also admitted to feeling somewhat powerless, because of course the decision had not been hers, but had been made by the administration above her without any input from the people who actually had to carry out the mandate. Chris was not initially aware of the severity of the emotional impact on herself for having to be what she would later coin as being a "hatchet man" either. The only bright spot, she told Marie, was that Nell, with her usual even tempered positive personality, had made things easier for her.

At least this was one time the rumor mill was a good thing, Chris thought. Nell had been prepared for what Chris was forced to do, and Chris felt it was harder on her than on Nell. Marie asked Chris to try something that Chris was not prepared for. Marie said, "Chris I think you are feeling guilty for following the decisions of our director. It was not your fault, so I am suggesting you forgive yourself, as it seems you feel personally responsible for a decision over which you had no control." Chris gasped. She realized how guilty she felt carrying out a decision from her supervisor. However, Marie's words rang true. She felt responsible both for letting Nell go and for the repercussions her staff would have to absorb from this decision. She realized being in middle management might mean carrying out more decisions over which she might not have control. They might include decisions that she was not given any chance to input into before they were made, either.

Chris let this realization sink in for a few seconds. Middle management seemed a more daunting role for her. Then she wondered how much influence even the director of nursing might have over certain budget cuts. She felt frustrated. Being in middle management in the nursing department at that moment felt like being the monkey in the middle. She had to follow what her supervisor told her to do. However, her staff saw her as the bad guy who either made the budget cut decision or at least was a part of it. Chris felt somewhat alone again, even with Marie standing right in front of her. She had to support the upper management decision, so she could not tell the staff she disagreed with it. On the other hand, if staff saw her as the bad guy she would have to mend bridges of trust with them, even though she had no control over this challenge.

She must have looked quite frustrated because Marie asked her what was wrong. When Chris shared her dilemma, Marie soberly agreed that middle management was one of the most difficult positions on the nursing leadership team. During tough times, such as carrying out a budget cut of a key position, it was especially tough. She gave Chris praise, however, for also being able to understand that probably the director herself had been given the edict either to cut unit secretaries or, at the very least, to remove from her nursing budget some specific amount. Her decision then could have come from her belief that the least detrimental cut would be unit secretaries. Either way, even the director of nursing in a hospital often has little input into matters such as budget cuts.

Chris contemplated this stark reality. She again realized being a nurse manager was not just about becoming a good leader, but being able to lead even when she had to deal with an adverse event, such as a staff reduction. She also felt the impact of such a decision, not just on the team and patient care, but on herself. Chris was a person who liked to build up people, a team, etc. Having to reduce staff and trying to help the team pick up the pieces of that extra work load was not what she planned for when she took the job. The humanitarian part of her was also hurting, because Nell was not just a "position cut," she was a human being. She was not just any human being, but a super nice member of her team. At that moment Chris again asked herself that question, *What am I doing?*

Chris pondered whether nursing management was right for her throughout that night. In the morning, however, she decided that even though it would be a rougher road than she had anticipated, she certainly would not quit, at least not when her team needed her. She decided to hold another meeting where she would invite the staff to talk about their feelings, as well as brain storm how to best deal with this challenge. She also chose to use the word *challenge* rather than *problem*, to stress that the team could retain some power to proactively deal with the issue.

Chris began the meeting by staying neutral about why the decision was made, in order to support her supervisor. Instead she stressed the positive—that although there was the need to cut the budget, no clinical staff were being laid off. She then asked the staff what they felt about losing Nell, their unit secretary. Ida admitted she really liked Nell and would miss her, and that she had trouble seeing who could fill her green front desk chair while still caring for patients. Charles shared seriously that he was concerned about the time it would take away from caring for his patients, pointing out that Nell had been able to multitask as well. Sarah said she thought it was not fair that someone who worked there so long could just be thrown out.

Darlene at first sat sullenly, quiet. Then she asked Chris if Chris really cared about Nell. Chris, shared honestly that it was very hard for her to have to tell Nell she was laid off. She added that even though Nell was gracious and left in the positive, professional way she always conducted herself, it felt awful to Chris. Darlene looked intently at Chris for a moment as if to try to get a feel for whether Chris was being honest or not. She must have begun to believe Chris, because her affect softened and she said more calmly, "I believe it was difficult for you." It seemed Darlene still had more to say by the way she gazed intently at Chris, but Chris thought better than to ask Darlene to extrapolate. She thanked the staff for sharing their feelings. She then asked for ideas on how to best try to re-allocate Nell's duties. The team was silent for a short while. Chris felt uneasy with the silence.

Chris then suggested that at least the front desk coverage would need to be dealt with that day. Ida was the first to respond. She suggested that the medication/treatment nurse could not cover between 8:00 a.m. and 10:00 a.m. and again 12:00 noon through 2:00 p.m. because she was preparing and passing medications, doing treatments, etc. Darlene nodded assent and mumbled, that report times 7:00 a.m. through 7:30 a.m. and 3:00 p.m. through 3:30 p.m. were times when charge nurses were not available. Charles and Sarah both chimed in with times, such as 7:30 through 11:00 a.m., when they were assisting patients who needed help to eat, checking vital signs, helping patients bathe and changing beds. Another difficult time for them was lunch time, 12:00 noon through 1:00 p.m. They both asked how they could be at the desk and be involved in needed patient care at the same time. Chris felt the sweat starting at the back of her neck again and her stomach was beginning to tie into a knot. How could she ask the staff to essentially be in two places at the same time?

Chris then asked each staff member how they could cover a total of one and a half hours each at the desk, because there would be six staff to do the coverage, including at least one part-time staff and Chris. The CNAs agreed that 11:00 a.m. to about 12:00 noon and 2:00 p.m. to 3:30 p.m. would be the best times for them to cover the desk. Darlene, somewhat reluctantly, admitted that as charge RN she was usually at the desk making out assignments, taking off doctors' orders, and doing discharges between 7:30 a.m. and around 11:00 a.m., with the exception of charge rounds and doing some patient care with the most seriously ill patients, hanging IVs, etc. Ida said 10:00 a.m. to 11:30 a.m. would work for her schedule, and Chris said usually she was able to be on the unit from 12:00 noon to either 1:30 or 2:00 p.m., as she had no managers' meetings at that time. Chris wrote down each staff member's preference, then handed the list to Darlene. She encouraged Darlene to assign the part-time CNA to cover at times when she had to leave the desk for short periods during the morning. She smiled at Darlene who again looked somewhat surprised that Chris would be willing to actually be part of the coverage solution. Chris was not sure if the last nurse manager was forced to face this type of dilemma. She did not remember a cut in staff being an issue during the three years she had been working for her present hospital. Nor did she remember staffing cuts being an issue in her last two positions, where she worked as a staff nurse.

Chris felt pleased with the outcome of this problem solving meeting. She again realized the staff had to move quickly through the nursing process. When she saw Marie that evening she shared that she felt good about opening the door for the staff to express their feelings, thoughts and concerns openly. She also felt good about the initial problem solving work that was done. While it appeared she had made some headway also with developing a working rapport with Darlene, the relationship seemed to go up and down during this process. Chris admitted that Darlene's non-verbal communication still made her feel uncomfortable sometimes.

Marie wisely asked, "Chris, do you think Darlene could be the emotional barometer for the team?" Chris became pensive for a moment, then a slow smile crept across her face. "Wow, what a more positive way to understand her behavior!" she exclaimed. Chris found herself taking a deep breath, and letting it out comfortably. If she could just distance her own emotional reaction to Darlene's seemingly negative looks, sighs and sometimes eye rolling by reminding herself that Darlene was the member of the team most in touch with her feelings, Chris could get a better feel for what the other team members might also be experiencing. Although Darlene was still the most difficult person for Chris to engage, she also could now see some value in her behavior, rather than just defining Darlene as her nemesis, or even a problem employee.

Chris felt pretty good overall about her problem solving meeting and mulled over Marie's suggestion to interpret Darlene's behavior as being the emotional barometer for the team. Whenever she was able to stay "in her head" while imagining herself dealing with Darlene's behavior, she did not get the now familiar knot in her stomach. She decided to try to just observe Darlene's behavior/reactions at the next staff meeting without making any judgment. Chris was honest with herself, however, that trying to stay neutral while dealing with behavior she considered to be somewhat belligerent at times would be difficult for her. Walking the tightrope between not allowing truly detrimental behavior within her team and interpreting some passive-aggressive communication as semi-open expression of true feelings would be tough. She decided, however, that one limit she wanted to set would be to reinforce that she expected the staff to talk to her about their concerns/issues/feelings and not talk behind her back.

Chris wondered how well the current problem solving would work and if the people who seemed to buy into the creation of the plan would actually embrace it. Since she had to be off the unit at times for a few hours at meetings or to do management paperwork in her small office, she knew she could not always personally supervise to make sure the plan was carried through. There was also the matter of re-delegating Nell's other duties.

Chris smiled as she remembered her first day on the unit as PM charge nurse. Nell had welcomed her and had showed her where to find nurses' notes as well as other important tools to do her job effectively. When visitors and physicians came to the unit, she always greeted them with a smile no matter how busy she might be, and she somehow never appeared rushed. Would Chris' remaining staff be able to keep up this high quality guest relations attitude while probably be feeling rushed to get their other duties completed? Chris knew this would be a wait-and-see proposition.

Nell, being the caring professional she was, had left a list of the other duties she formerly performed with Chris. Tearing down old charts from discharged patients and preparing new charts in anticipation of their vacillating patient daily turnover in itself would be time consuming. Writing out lab requests and following through to ensure labs were completed would be another challenge.

Chris talked with Marie about this dilemma. Marie became pensive for a moment, then asked Chris, "Do you lead only the day shift?" Chris blinked a few times. Why hadn't she thought of redistributing whatever she could to all three shifts? She knew the shift that had the least patient care contact tended to be the night shift. However, at first she felt somewhat stymied. She could ask the night shift to "stuff" new charts. However, if her unit was full, all of the charts would be in use, with the exception of two extras available in case a three-ringed chart binder became damaged.

She thought a bit, then concluded it should not be too hard to requisition an extra dozen patient chart binders. In that way she could ensure there would always be enough of them ready for even the most prolific day of admissions. She also reasoned that there was no law that said a chart had to be broken down in a short time when a patient left. There could be a place designated to pile old charts until the night shift could dismantle them. Chris felt some of the burden could in this way be lifted from the day shift.

However, now Chris was more acutely aware of how strong personalities reacted to change. She also realized that so far she had neither included the night shift in problem solving, nor had she even thought that the evening shift might need some help dealing with reallocating Nell's duties. She had just assumed her evening staff would figure out how to cover the desk from 3:30—7:30 p.m. At home that evening Chris vowed she would talk with her evening staff the next day, but first she would need to come in early, before the 7:00 a.m. report, to discuss re-allocating the chart filling-and-emptying issue with the night staff.

Chris decided to call Marie that evening, as she was aware there was another strong personality who worked the night shift who would have to be on board with the extra workload in order for the transition of these duties to be at least relatively smooth. Marie asked Chris what her major fear was about presenting this issue to Deborah, the night charge RN, and the night staff. Chris responded that Deborah came across to her as authoritative, and when Chris had worked with her in the past, Deborah had usually gotten upset with the previous nurse manager whenever a change occurred that involved her shift. The current situation would not just be a change, but would require additional work from that group.

Marie then asked Chris, "What is your worst fantasy about what might happen when you present this challenge?" Chris laughed a little after picturing Deborah blowing up at her yelling and saying she just plain would not do it. Marie then asked her to imagine how she might like someone else to start off a conversation that presents a new challenge that would require some extra effort from her. Chris thought for a moment, then offered that maybe she would like to know why the additional workload was needed and why from her.

Marie asked, "And what about the why? I mean, what happened that was not in your control, that made this additional work necessary?" Chris got the message, and said that first she would let the night shift know, if they had not yet heard, that their Nell had been laid off due to a budget cut. She would share how the day and evening shift now had to take over several duties, including covering the desk while trying to keep up quality patient care. Only then would she ask for the night shift's help to deal with this challenge. By letting them know the full picture of what happened and also that other shifts would be taking on more responsibilities too, she hoped that Deborah would see that the whole staff needed to pull together to effectively deal with the change. She then planned to explain what she needed them to do, and that she already had ordered a dozen more chart binders to facilitate having enough resources for them to effectively carry out the new duty of "stuffing" charts in anticipation of new patients being admitted to their unit. She thought she could engage Deborah further by asking her where she and her staff wanted to store discharged patients' charts from the day and evening shifts in a way that would ensure their patients' confidentiality but also be convenient for the night shift staff to work with them.

Marie restated, "In other words, you would let them know the whole picture, their part needed to successfully deal with re-allocation of the work, and engage them in problem solving." Chris pondered for a moment, then replied to Marie that it did seem like the most positive way to approach a difficult situation with a potentially difficult employee. She also shared that she always liked feeling she had some control over situations, especially those that didn't always seem as if she had any control over the decision that caused them.

Chris came in fifteen minutes before report, after calling Deborah to let her know they needed to have a brief problem solving meeting. Deborah, like Darlene, used non-verbal communication to show her likes and dislikes pretty clearly. When Chris arrived on the unit, Deborah looked at her suspiciously. Chris just smiled and began by explaining what happened. She reassured the night staff that she had talked to Nell and that Nell was doing all right, even seeing the decision as facilitating her early retirement. She then shared how the other shifts had taken on parts of Nell's responsibilities. Deborah interrupted before Chris could voice what she needed from the night shift. She said in a curt tone, sounding impatient to Chris, "So what do you want from us?" Chris took a deep breath, as she felt that familiar knot starting to tie in her stomach.

She looked directly at Deborah and replied in the calmest tone she could muster. "We need your help preparing charts for new patients and breaking down charts from discharged patients from the day and evening shifts." She then kept silent for a few seconds, which seemed like several minutes, in order to let the night shift charge nurse reply and share her thoughts/feelings openly. Deborah gave a deep sigh and mumbled something Chris did not understand. She waited another few seconds, then asked Deborah where she would like to put the discharged charts that would be safe and yet convenient for her staff. Deborah did not reply right away, but did look around the nursing desk/office space. "I guess we could put them on the back counter, in a bin marked 'discharged charts'." Chris then asked Deborah what she felt would be the safest way to make sure lab works had been done from the day before, and were marked for the physician to read on the front of charts. Deborah at first looked as if she were going to say something—not too nice—but did not. She did say she was not sure the night shift should be checking labs that were done on the day shift because they might need the attention of the physician before the next day.

Chris thought a second or two and agreed with Deborah that this duty probably would need to be one that was checked by the charge nurse before the end of each shift. Days and evenings were the ones that usually had blood draws and other lab work done. Therefore checking before the end of each shift would ensure timely reporting of abnormal labs to the physicians. Deborah appeared surprised. She looked again like she wanted to say something, but didn't.

Chris thanked Deborah and the night shift for their support during this tough time. One of the CNAs (Carol) then volunteered to be the person to stuff charts when she was on duty, as she previously had been a unit secretary before becoming a certified nurse assistant. Another CNA (Stan) said he was fast at breaking down charts and did not think this would be a major issue. Deborah looked surprised at her staff who seemed to quickly problem solve the issue without adding more burden to her night shift nursing duties. Her tone and facial expression softened and she told Chris the night shift would do their part to deal with Nell's loss. She then also shared she was glad the layoff was not too hard emotionally on Nell, as even though they did not work together she heard Nell was a really nice person and a dedicated staff member. Chris agreed Nell was both nice and a valued team member and that she also missed Nell's positive way of interacting with everybody.

Chris felt this meeting went well. She knew she would have to follow up to make sure the charts actually were stuffed every day, because she now was more acutely aware that people sometimes seem to buy into a quick change, but in the long run they may not actually do what is needed of them. Chris also knew she had one more shift team to work with regarding this change. That team, she realized, no longer was hers because there was a new charge nurse who started when Chris went to the day shift. The other qualified RN who could have become permanent charge nurse did want that position as she planned to reduce to part-time in the near future. Therefore, the leader now was really not known to Chris, as the former nurse manager hired her. Irene was a young, high energy person in her mid twenties which, Chris was aware, meant she might be a person who did not stay too long in one place.

Chris had called Irene the evening before to let her know they needed to meet for a problem solving session regarding re-allocating Nell's duties from 3:30 to 7:30 p.m. When Chris came into the meeting room, Irene smiled and said rapidly that they wanted to know what Chris needed them to do. Chris again began by letting the evening staff know what had happened, and that both the day and night shift had taken some of Nell's duties and re-allocated them. She shared that the day shift had chosen to make a schedule so staff members knew when they needed to cover the desk, and that the night shift had taken on making new charts and breaking down discharged charts.

She asked Irene what the evening shift had done in the last two days since Nell left to cover the desk. Irene beamed, "Oh, we just kept an eye on the desk and if someone was not there, another staff member would sit at the desk until I got back. It really wasn't any problem." Chris was quiet for a few seconds, because she wanted to blurt out something like, "What were you thinking? You need a system to deal with this, not just hope someone will be there to do the job!" However, she thought better than to be quite that honest. Instead she calmly asked how that had worked for the staff, visitors and patients. The older nurse, Sandy, who was planning to go part-time soon, looked at the floor. The two CNAs who were present looked at each other, and one rolled his eyes. Chris could tell from these non-verbals that the PM staff was not too sure things were working "just fine".

Chris suggested Irene might want to schedule someone at the desk for an hour or so in order for each staff member to know when he or she was responsible to cover it. Irene looked hurt, as if she felt Chris had criticized her. Chris smiled at her and simply stated that this plan seemed to work for the day shift pretty well. That way the staff would not feel nervous trying to check to see if someone else was at the desk, nor would one staff member feel the need to stay at the desk for an extended period of time waiting for someone to relieve him or her. This could help avoid one person taking on more than their share of time and putting them behind in their other duties. The other three staff members nodded, and Irene took note.

Irene quickly agreed to assign people to half-hour increments, and she herself would take on about one and a half hours since she had to be at the desk doing charge nurse paperwork anyway. Chris complimented Irene for how quickly she responded to this need, adding that she appreciated Irene for taking the lion's share of the responsibility. Irene then smiled and no longer looked stressed. However, Chris also knew that Irene might be going along with her suggestion because Irene seemed to be the personality type that liked to be liked. Chris was a little wary of how quickly Irene agreed both to assigning a person to the front desk and to taking on the majority of the responsibility. She may have just wanted Chris to feel like she was doing what her nurse manager suggested. Chris would wait and see. She also was getting better at picking up non-verbal communication and would keep an eye on the evening staff to see if there was any further negative non-verbal communication over the next few days.

Chris again realized just how much effort it took to deal with different age groups, communication styles, etc. and to get the three different shifts to work as one team. Nursing management was more complicated than she had anticipated, but she thought she was making some headway. Chris was also glad she had Marie to mentor her through this transition period. She did not know if she could do this all alone.

What did Chris learn about dealing with changes?

1. Changes occur—sometimes rapidly—in the workplace today, not giving the manager time to prepare her staff to deal with them.
2. It is important to let the staff see a manager as a person who cares when a loss occurs.
3. If staff seem to accept a change too readily and don't react with any emotion, it could mean they are experiencing a form of the grief response. People experiencing a loss often start out in shock/disbelief. During that initial phase of a grief response, they frequently show little overt reaction. This can easily be mistaken for an acceptance of the change.
4. If someone on the staff expresses either verbal or, in the case of Darlene, non-verbal anger or other perceived negative emotions, begin to view that person as the emotional barometer for the team, rather than a malcontent.
5. The manager can engage the staff by asking them to share their reactions, concerns, etc. openly, without fear of repercussions.
6. A good leader elicits staff's ideas and other input in order to problem solve dealing with a change, such as the one Chris had to face redistributing Nells' workload.
7. If the whole team is actually based on three different shifts, it is important to engage all shifts affected by the change.
8. Other shift leadership people, such as Darlene, Irene and

Deborah, all need to buy into any plans that are made in order for them to succeed.

9. Various communication and personality styles have different needs, as Chris will learn further in chapter five, so attempting to engage every member of the team exactly the same way may not work.

10. Ideally, preparing staff for major changes before they are implemented helps both the manager and staff better plan an effective strategy and makes the change less stressful. In the next chapter, Chris will be given some lead time to deal with another change before it occurs. See how this lead time can make a difference in the response of the staff and the amount of stress it causes for the team.

CHAPTER FOUR:

Prepare Staff for Major Changes

Chris was afraid of what might be about to happen. Getting a call from the director of nursing asking that she attend an urgent full management meeting was anxiety provoking for a new manager. The director stated that the chief executive officer (CEO) would be presenting another change he declared was "necessary". Chris knew this probably meant another budget cut that could make a negative impact on patient care—and her team.

Chris arrived a few minutes early for the meeting. She sat across from Marie so she could try to read her non-verbal responses to the CEO's announcements. The CEO entered the room in what Chris thought was a brusque manner. His facial muscles appeared tense and his face was somewhat red. Chris had an ominous feeling before he spoke. The CEO's tone was stern and matter-of-fact. He stated that it had come to his attention that many staff arrived late to work and he suspected some left early as well. Due to how much money was wasted paying staff when they were not working, he decided to initiate a time clock system. That way the hospital could also reduce the financial staff by the one who was checking hand-written time cards. He stated that these actions were necessary to re-establish financial stability, as was his first decision to do away with the "extraneous group" of unit secretaries. He did not ask for anyone's opinion or input about his decision.

Chris looked to her mentor, Marie, for support. Marie kept a poker face through the brief pronouncement, but the look in her eyes, Chris thought, was a tacit way of letting Chris know Marie understood the ramifications of putting professional nurses on a time clock. Marie's affect,

Chris felt, was a cue also to how she should respond—or in this case not respond at all—emotionally.

The DON. (director of nursing), Susan, tentatively asked the CEO if he meant the professional nursing staff would also have to use a time clock. The CEO shot back a look toward the DON that literally scared Chris. In what to Chris sounded like a sarcastic tone, the CEO snarled, "Professional is a matter of opinion, and when I say staff, I mean all staff!" Susan looked down at the table in front of her. Chris did not know Susan well, but she seemed quiet and not too assertive to her. The nurse manager wanted to say what she felt—that this change, especially on top of the recent re-allocation of her team's workload, would probably cause a backlash. However, she thought it wiser to stay quiet.

After the meeting, Chris approached Marie, who listened sympathetically. She gave Chris positive feedback for refraining from showing an emotional response to the new CEO's style, and announcement. Chris expressed concerns about her perception that the CEO might not respect the value of the nursing department in their facility. Dealing with a top level executive who came across as an autocratic leader, along with a DON who did not seem to stand up for nursing, was a difficult combination for Chris to swallow. Again she questioned herself as to why she had taken this job.

Chris then realized the new CEO had not given them a time frame for this change. Maybe she would have at least a few weeks to prepare the staff and let them get used to the idea before expecting them to punch a time clock. She did not look forward to presenting this second shock to her team so soon after they seemed to be effectively dealing with the first one.

Chris shared her concerns with Marie. Marie reasoned that since a new two week pay period had just begun, they probably had at least the next two weeks to prepare the staff to deal with the change. Marie also agreed to talk with the Human Resources director to find out the exact date the change was due to go into effect. Chris thought that was a creative way to get the information she needed to prepare the unit staff, as neither she nor Marie wanted to put Susan in harm's way by asking her to approach the CEO again. Chris thought sometimes ignorance was in fact bliss, as she knew she would be the person targeted for an angry response from at least two of her staff members because they might believe she had some input into making this decision that would very probably be perceived as an insult to their professionalism.

Chris waited for Marie to call her to get the details of the change before approaching her staff. She knew the more information she had, the more she would be able to prepare the team for this new challenge. Chris also had her own feelings about time clocks. She had only worked one facility briefly that expected nurses to punch a clock, and she felt it was degrading to her professionalism. Therefore Chris took some time to process her own feelings about this perceived devaluation of her chosen profession because she knew she had to come across in at least a neutral manner to the staff. It would not be easy for her, since she disagreed with this decision just as she did not view Nell's position as an extraneous one. She felt uncomfortable with the CEO's style of both making decisions and imposing emotionally charged changes on the staff, especially the first one where he gave no warning to the managers who were expected to carry out the layoff. At least in this case there would be a window of change of no less than two weeks, until the beginning of the next pay period.

Marie called Chris later that evening at her home. She had the details Chris needed to begin the process of getting the staff to accept punching a time clock. Marie shared that at least they would be able to use their identification badges to badge in rather than just punch a time card. This minor difference might be more acceptable to professional staff. There was also a window of seven minutes for staff to badge in before their shift started. They could leave the unit and badge out up to seven minutes after their shift ended as well. Chris asked what would happen if a staff member badged out more than seven minutes late, and Marie cautioned that the person would be paid fifteen minutes overtime. However, getting paid the overtime would be a black mark against the staff member unless the overtime was approved by a supervisor or manager at the time the person stayed over. When Marie had asked where the time clocks would be located, the Human Resources director replied that he was not sure. She suggested there be one located outside each unit or at least one per floor between two units. The Human Resources director, who Chris only knew slightly, seemed like an upbeat and friendly person. She hoped he was also open to suggestions, such as the excellent one Marie had given him. The HR director also shared with Marie that he was not sure exactly when the time clock system would be implemented, but thought it would be soon, since the new CEO tended to make changes rapidly.

Not knowing where the time clock or clocks might be located placed an extra stress on Chris. She knew at least two of her staff would ask this question and felt plans should be more concrete before they actually made this change. However, knowing how the informal communication network worked in a hospital setting, i.e., gossip, she also thought she better have a meeting and let her staff know at least as much as she knew before they heard it through the grapevine. Chris therefore decided to take just a few minutes in the morning with the night and day shift and again to talk with the evening staff at change of shift the next day.

Chris discussed how she might approach her staff, to try to help allay the brunt of the negative impact she anticipated it would have on the team. One idea Marie suggested was to use a less emotional term to deal with *punching* a time clock. Since staff, she found out from the Human Resources director, would be using their new identification badges to punch in, she suggested using the words *badge in* instead. Chris thought this minor difference in description of this new expectation might cause slightly less emotional impact. She and Marie also discussed how to present at least one positive spin on it, such as it was faster than filling out and signing time cards, and there would be less likelihood of any pay errors from the accounting department. They decided Chris would not stress that this change would cause the loss of a job in the accounting department. They felt it might bring up more grief feelings due to the unit staff's recent loss of Nell.

Chris took a deep breath when she entered the report room the next morning to help loosen the knot in her stomach. She thought it best to keep the tone calm and professional for the night/day shift emergency meeting she had announced the night before. In her mirror the previous evening she had practiced letting staff know in a matter of fact way what was going to happen soon. However, she did not feel she would be very convincing. She had also called ahead to make sure there would be a pot of coffee and water for tea available to try to create a somewhat warmer atmosphere. Nothing she had done to prepare, however, seemed to allay her fears that this change would be perceived as being very unpopular with her staff in general and she expected an angry backlash from at least two nurses.

Chris began the meeting by stating the facts as she had them at that time. She used the words *badge in* rather than *punch in* and stressed the positive spin. Then she explained the change would happen in the near future, but no sooner than after this next pay period. She then stayed quiet for a few seconds—that felt like hours—waiting for staff's response. Darlene, not surprisingly, had seen through the ploy of putting a more palatable label on punching in. She said sourly, "You mean nurses will be expected to punch a time clock?" The rest of the staff looked from Darlene to Chris, awaiting Chris' reply. Chris took another deep breath before answering.

She knew Darlene was one of the brightest members of the unit's team, and at that moment realized she had both the formal title of permanent charge nurse and possibly the informal position of leader of the dayshift part of her team. She needed to choose her words carefully, because even though staff probably were not aware of it, she had no power to change upper management's decision. Chris decided to stress the benefits of using a time clock, rather than emphasizing that most nurses she knew worked at hospitals where they were able to sign in and out, but only a few where the badge system was in place. The ones who worked for hospitals where time clocks were instituted were also friends who had told her that they felt nurses were treated with disrespect in other areas as well. She did not want to share that information with her staff, however, as her goal right now was to get her team to swallow a decision that left a sour taste in her mouth.

Chris began by asking what punching a time clock meant to the staff. Darlene immediately answered she felt doing so was treating professionals like factory workers. Other members of the day shift and night shift teams nodded their heads in support. Chris acknowledged the staff's feelings, while reinforcing that, per the CEO, the professional nursing staff as well as all other employees, including management staff, would be badging in, so no one group of people would be singled out. The positive, Chris continued, would be that it was fast, easy and would cut down on any human errors that could occur when someone writes out a time card, and then another person has to read it and enter the data into a computer. The staff looked pensive, and Chris sensed the tone in the room felt less tense.

Darlene looked at Deborah, the night shift charge nurse, and they both shrugged. At least, Chris thought with relief, the two strongest members of her team, and the ones that could create the most tension and dissonance, were considering both sides of the issue and becoming more neutral than she had anticipated. However, Chris was getting savvy enough to know an initial response to a change of this emotional magnitude might have more repercussions down the road, especially if other upper management decisions that could be perceived as slighting the nursing department occurred in the near future. Chris was not at all sure this would be the last money saving idea the CEO would come up with, while her staff was still trying to deal with the last two decisions he made. Chris was also not so sure she wanted to be part of a management team where the top nurse leader seemed to be afraid even to make a comment or give her input to the CEO.

Chris decided to share her concerns with Marie after talking with the PM shift at the 3:00 p.m. meeting. Chris anticipated that Irene, the new evening shift charge nurse, would acquiesce to the new procedure without much trouble. She was right. When Chris mentioned that the staff would need to badge in within the near future, she waited for a response. Irene just smiled and asked if they needed special badges. Chris stated that new badges would be issued, and again stressed how it would save time and the possibility of human error. Irene just continued to smile, while some of the rest of the staff looked at Chris with serious expressions. Chris again invited people to share their feelings about this new change. One of her loyal, usually quieter staff members, an LPN named Clara, asked Chris whether nursing had done something wrong, such as too many of them coming late to work, for the staff to be "punished by making them punch a time clock."

Chris felt relieved that someone had addressed the "elephant in the middle of the living room" so to speak. She reassured the staff that she had not heard that nursing was being singled out due to some of the nursing staff possibly being late for work. She reiterated that the CEO had stated that all staff, including management staff from all departments, would be badging in so the change would be a fair one across the board. She also emphasized that the decision had more to do with saving staff's time and reducing the chance of errors. Clara shared she had been underpaid once a few months ago due to an error from the financial department. She agreed that using a machine to keep staff's hours might cut down on payroll errors.

Chris was glad no one asked yet about the details of how early they could badge in or how late they could badge out before they would accidentally be paid fifteen minutes overtime. Her staff usually were on time, but many stayed up to one half hour overtime, without asking for compensation, to complete charting or care of a patient. One of Chris' friends who worked where the time clock was instituted told her how she was chastised for accidentally badging in a minute early, when the time clock where she worked was habitually two to three minutes fast. She always set her watch three minutes ahead and badged in when her watch said five minutes before the hour her shift started, but to her horror, after badging in one day, the clock read eight minutes before the hour. They were not to badge in earlier than seven minutes before their shift began, or the time clock would automatically pay them fifteen minutes extra time. She was threatened with being "written up" if she came in early again. Her friend found herself getting anxious about coming to work for a long while after that, and rushing through her work to ensure she did not badge out late, either.

Chris really needed to talk to Marie both to vent her feelings and to plan how to keep herself and her staff safe. Even admitting that she felt unsafe for herself—as she knew she would be punished if her staff did not follow the new guidelines that would soon be put into place—caused the familiar knot to tighten in her stomach. Marie looked serious when Chris approached her. Marie admitted she too had friends who worked with time clocks, and some of them also shared similar experiences to Chris' friend. She advised Chris to warn her staff about what was considered unacceptable badging times, including coming in too early and leaving a little late, which she had just clarified with the Human Resources director, before the change actually went into effect.

Chris was not sure if she should just place a memo in each staff member's mailbox to let them know what the acceptable in and out time ranges would be when the badging process began. The positive of using a memo would be that all the staff would have the same information, and misinformation would be kept at a minimum. It would also give her staff time to pre-plan how to arrive at work within the seven minute window. She knew a few of her staff lived several miles from the hospital and traffic was at times unpredictable, especially for those on the afternoon shift. Although it was rare, at least one staff member called more than once saying she was stuck in traffic and might be up to fifteen minutes late. Chris feared any deviation from the new CEO's dictates would cause repercussions, so she decided not to add that a staff member should call ahead if he or she were being unavoidably detained, because it probably would not make any difference. That staff member would be considered tardy. She also feared that this type of leader might force her to "write up" people, even those who had valid reasons for a rare tardy incident.

Chris was not at all sure she wanted to stay a leader in this organization if upper management should become what she felt could be considered dictatorial. She was in general a person who cooperated with reasonable requests and changes. However, the first two this CEO had imposed seemed to her to show that neither was he in touch with the needs of her department, nor were his requests necessarily in the best interest of the patients being served.

Chris kept the memo brief, and matter-of-fact in tone. She invited any staff member who had questions about it to talk with her individually. She vowed to answer any questions in a matter-of-fact manner. Chris knew that despite her disagreement with this decision, she had to maintain her position as a nurse leader within the chain of leadership. If she let her staff know her true feelings about this new CEO and his negative attitude toward her department, it would only cause more stress for her staff, as well as jeopardize her job. At this point, she felt she was "between a rock and a hard place," having to go along with what she knew would be another unpopular decision that would affect the morale of her team, and needing to present a positive attitude while carrying out the decision.

Once Chris hand-delivered the memo to each staff member's mailbox to ensure they all had the same information, she waited for a response. No response could feel good for the moment, but Chris also knew how people who felt disempowered tended to go underground. Her new evening charge nurse was a person who would most likely use a passive-aggressive approach. That way she could appear to support her nurse manager, but once Chris left the room, Irene would be almost certain to bad mouth her. Chris actually felt more positive about dealing with Darlene and Deborah, whom she could count on to overtly question, and also possibly challenge, this new dictate. At least she would hear their concerns to her face, rather than just feel an icy air from other staff members Irene might have complained to behind her back. Funny, Chris thought, I was more afraid of dealing with the nurses I perceived as being assertive, powerful, or even sometimes a bit aggressive. However, now I realize that talking about the concerns up-front and honestly is the only way to actually get to the real issues and deal with them.

Chris decided she should talk to Marie about setting out some guidelines to help her staff openly express their needs and feelings without aggression. She knew she needed to reach out for extra support, because she was feeling more and more like one of the old Roman messengers who sometimes were shot by the emperor if they brought bad news.

What Did Chris learn about dealing with major changes?

1. Changes may occur rapidly, and two emotionally packed changes such as the ones Chris and her team experienced can compound their stress level and make it more difficult to adjust.
2. The second change allowed some lag time so Chris and her team could be more prepared to deal with it.
3. Since badging in was also a professionalism issue for her nursing staff and herself, Chris needed first to identify her own feelings, then try to diffuse the bad taste it left in her mouth before introducing it to the staff. Chris did this both internally and externally by talking it over with her mentor, Marie.
4. Before introducing the change to her staff, Chris also had time to gather as much information as possible. Imagine if she had just relayed the bare essence of what the CEO shared. She would be barraged by questions, such as what the time parameters were for badging in and out, and when the change would occur. Although she still did not have an exact date the process would start, she at least knew it would not be the same day, as Nell's departure had been.
5. Chris questioned whether she wanted to stay in this organization due to the style the CEO was exhibiting, expecting more possibly rapidly occurring decisions that would have high emotional impact on the staff as well as possible serious repercussions for their patients.
6. Chris kept a neutral attitude when presenting the change, despite her own disagreement with the idea. She learned that being in middle management sometimes meant she would be the bearer of bad news, while she had little or nothing to do with actually making the decision.
7. Chris utilized the support of her mentor Marie several times

to help gather and present the most information possible about the change and to help deal with her own feelings. She then came across as more supportive of upper management to the staff, despite feeling disrespected as a professional herself.

8. Chris asked herself the same question many new nurse managers, as well as supervisors, and DONs, often ask themselves when they encounter the management style this CEO was presenting. The good news is that management styles don't have to be the same all the time. This CEO could become less autocratic once he felt more secure in his new post. However, Chris' current priority was to deal with her own anxiety and negative feelings, much like a parent who does not agree with a limit set by the other parent has to. She knew that despite her personal feelings and beliefs, she needed to present a united front with the CEO and DON when interacting with her staff.

9. Both personality and management styles play a role in how well members of a team adapt to a change as well as how much emotional intelligence a top leader may display, which sets the tone for an organization. In the next chapter, Chris will learn more about different personality styles and how to engage each type.

CHAPTER FIVE:

Employ Individual Approaches with Different Personality Styles

Although early in her management career, Chris already was aware there was no such thing as a "cookie cutter" approach to dealing with diverse staff. She was able to recognize which communication style her different staff members were generally employing, their generational priorities and that there may be some cultural diversity issues as well at times with her staff. She read about the DISC personality styles , McClure (2007) and began talking to Marie about how she could try to tailor her approaches to each of the styles she thought were being employed by different staff members. Marie smiled broadly at her protégé. She complimented Chris on doing her homework and researching a practical system of organizing personality traits into four major personality style categories, each with its own special needs.

She reminded Chris that there were actually about fifteen combination styles, in reality, but that just identifying the four major ones would help Chris get the basics so she could try to meet the critical needs of each style. This knowledge could also help her more effectively communicate with them and better engage the staff to cooperate with her as their leader. Marie and Chris discussed how each personality style had specific needs and fears. For example, the *dominant* (D) style needed to feel in control and feared the loss of control. Chris immediately recognized both Darlene and Deborah; the off shift charge nurses seemed to use this style. It made more sense to Chris after studying the dominant style why both of them were the most verbal sharing negative feelings about changes that affected patient care (loss of Nell) and that could be perceived as a blow to their professionalism (having to badge in and out at work).

Dominants or drivers (D), according to the Institute for Motivational Living, Inc in their article *DISC Profile Characteristics 2009,* communicate in a direct manner and they are problem solvers and risk takers. They are valuable to the team because they are innovative, bottom-line organizers who are not afraid to challenge the status quo. However, they can also become argumentative, and can overstep their authority. On a positive note, they actually don't like routines and enjoy changes and challenges. However, they also have a fear of being taken advantage of, and will react—like the two dominants/drivers on Chris' team—when they feel this is happening to them.

Ida and Irene, Chris reasoned, were probably *influence* (I) personality type people. Both of them were enthusiastic, optimistic, talkative and persuasive. They could be valuable to the team in that they were more creative problem solvers, and could motivate others through encouragement. They also made good peace makers and negotiators for conflict resolution. Chris was aware that these people could also respond to stress more emotionally than others, as they showed their emotions more overtly, wanted to be liked, were not always attentive to details and tended to listen only when it was convenient. Since their greatest fear is rejection, they might seem to be going along with unpopular changes, while really disagreeing with them. Thus these people might be the most likely of all the personality styles to "backbite" rather than express feelings, dissatisfaction, etc. directly.

Stan, Sarah and Sandy were *steady* or *steadiness* (S) personality types. They were good listeners, team players naturally friendly and predictable. They were reliable and dependable, loyal to the team and complied with authority figures. They were patient, empathic and good at helping to reconcile conflicts proactively. However, Chris was also aware this style resists change so it may take them a longer time to adjust. They may hold grudges, be sensitive to criticism and have some difficulty establishing priorities. She was acutely aware they had a fear of loss of security. Chris knew she would need to take some extra time with this group of people to support them during the two changes that were already made by the new CEO.

Clara, Charles and Carol were all *conscientious/compliance* (C) style people. They were quieter, more analytical, careful and precise. They held themselves to high standards of performance and made decisions carefully, based on facts. C style people give value to a team as they are even tempered, thorough in carrying out their assignments, and have a reality based perspective. They gather, test and sometimes criticize information, and tend to make decisions more slowly as they consider all aspects of a situation, etc. However, they need clear-cut boundaries for their relationships, and seem almost bound by procedures. They can get bogged down in details, possibly losing the whole picture in the process. Compliance types prefer not to verbalize their feelings and will often give in rather than argue a point. Their greatest fear is being criticized. Therefore, Chris knew she would have a challenge helping this part of her team deal with change because they would need time to analyze why the changes occur and what impact the changes would make on them. When they did not agree with a decision, they would probably deal with it internally. They would very likely have difficulty sharing more than a cursory criticism of the decisions, and might also express a tentative disagreement with a dead pan affect. Chris knew she had to watch both what she said and how she said it with this subgroup, because they were the most sensitive to taking what she shared as a criticism.

Chris came to the realization that both of her dominants tended also to use the kinesthetic style of communication, although she was not too sure that Darlene was a pure dominant. She observed that the influencers were inclined to talk rapidly and use a lot of visual language. Since they tended to like to persuade people to their way of thinking, it made sense to Chris that they would talk fast and quite a lot. Security oriented people, on the other hand, talked little, more softly and used "thinking" words. Therefore, Chris reasoned, this personality type also might have deep feelings about issues but don't express them. In addition, they seemed to have the most trouble expressing their concerns. In some systems, though, it was unsafe to let people in authority know what you were truly thinking or feeling.

Although Chris was not an openly feeling person, she had taken a stress management class to help her get in touch with her body's reactions to stressful situations. It helped when she identified she could feel sweat on the back of her neck when she had anticipatory stress. In addition, when she experienced an immediate threat to her self-esteem, she could now feel the knot right after it formed in her stomach. It was not so easy for her to express deep feelings, although she could talk easily to others or in front of a group. In fact, Chris knew, she had to consciously slow down at times.

She was also working on listening more and talking less when interacting with others in general. She knew that taking her time and actually sharing details and encouraging clarifying questions with the conscientious style people were necessary to meet their need for gathering all the details. Since they also tended to have somewhat lower voices and were slower making decisions based on getting the "whole picture," she reasoned that they probably used the auditory mode of communication most often, as they were good listeners. Chris remembered that while this style did not talk much when they shared a suggestion or asked a question related to an issue, their input was usually profound. She suddenly felt a greater respect for those who took time to process information more thoroughly than most of her team before responding.

After reading about these personality styles, Chris took another personal inventory. She surprised herself when she could admit that even though Darlene and Deborah were so direct she felt intimidated by them at times, she might have to put more energy into getting real buy-in to change from the other three styles.

Chris realized she needed to look deeper inside herself and maybe ask her mentor which style Marie thought Chris used most often, as she was not quite sure. Marie smiled proudly at her protégé, and complimented Chris for taking this important but often uncomfortable step. Looking inside oneself was sometimes hard to do, and is even scary to some people. Marie was thoughtful for a moment, then she shared that although the most accurate way to really know your own style is to take a DISC assessment profile, it was her opinion that Chris was probably a combination style, called a *creative*. Chris asked what that meant and Marie explained it was basically a combination style of dominant and conscientious. Chris looked pensive, then nodded. Remembering the two styles, she could relate to both wanting to make things happen in a positive way—i.e., wanting to have some control over decisions—and being careful, analytical and sensitive, expecting high standards from herself and others. She recognized that her biggest fears were, in fact, loss of control and being criticized..

Chris suddenly had another *aha* moment that she shared with Marie. It hit her that there really were no good or bad employees, only a variety of people with different needs and fears. Since people used different modes to communicate that included various rates of speed, amount of talking, varying degrees of emotion being shown, and wording that reflected whether they were more visual, auditory, kinesthetic (feeling) or thinking oriented, they might easily be misunderstood by people who usually used a different mode to communicate. As complicated as that realization seemed to be, Chris felt strangely as if she could be a little more pro-active, at least with her staff. She wished she felt more like she could have an impact on the administration above her, though.

Chris again questioned whether managing in this particular system was the best place for her to be, as presently she felt she had little control over the decisions that were being made by the new CEO, and she had to admit she did not want to be criticized by her staff for having to carry out his decisions. She wondered whether she could consider herself to be a "difficult employee," as she was having a lot of trouble wanting to support and stand behind edicts she did not think were in the best interest of either the patients or her staff. Chris shared her concerns with her mentor. Marie, with a somewhat sad affect, let Chris know that while she also had concerns about a pattern that might be developing of making quick decisions to deal with "bottom line" issues (saving money) she had weathered several administrations in her long career. Often, once the initial perceived financial emergency passed, the new person in power became less controlling.

She shared that once a new leader she had worked with had even seemed to do a near 180 degree turn, and started encouraging input from middle managers—and even staff in some areas—regarding dealing with challenges. However, she also admitted that this had only happened once in her career. More often, Marie added, the autocratic CEO would seem to "burn out" fairly quickly and leave the organization. Marie encouraged Chris to hang in there and put her emphasis on helping her diverse team deal with the challenges at hand and growing a team spirit. Marie stressed that one of the most disastrous things a new manager can do was to talk badly about the administration above her to the staff. Instead, she encouraged Chris to spend some time looking for areas she could control on a day to day basis, and treat her staff in such a way that they would be more likely to feel valued and respected. In this way the fears Chris was experiencing—of loss of control and of being criticized—could be abated at least when she was on her unit.

Chris thought for a moment of the *Serenity Prayer*, Niebuhr (1943) that people in the 12 step programs used, part of which said something about the wisdom to know the difference between things she could and could not control. While she could not control the CEO's decisions, how he presented them to the middle managers to then present to the staff, nor his seeming disrespect for her profession, she could control how she felt and acted when she was on her unit interacting with her staff. She could come in with a positive attitude, remembering to smile and greet each staff member, recognizing them as important, valued people. She could engage the staff in brain storming and problem solving how to carry out the mandates of the CEO in a way that was pro-active. She could give encouragement to her staff and recognition of their hard work, including modifying what they did to fill the void left by Nell, and figure out a way to reward staff who consistently stayed within the on-time guidelines for coming in and leaving work. Chris felt somewhat less stressed as she considered these options, and more in control—of herself. After all she reasoned, there really was no one/nothing else she could really control, except herself.

Chris made some mental notes of ways she could approach her staff, knowing many of them had different personality styles, and remembering they also communicated using different communication modes. This management gig was more complicated than she first imagined, but she vowed she would put in the effort to become a success. She also had to remind herself that becoming a really accomplished manager would probably take time. Since patience was not yet one of her virtues, Chris knew she would have to continuously self monitor to make sure her impatience did not show through when dealing with the management challenges she knew would continue to be forthcoming.

What did Chris learn about engaging different personality styles?

1. There are four major personality types with combinations creating a total of fifteen per the DISC assessment profile in the *Disc Classic 2.0 report for Helen Thamm*, 2007.
2. Chris was able to identify which major personality style several of her staff portrayed.
3. She realized she needed to utilize different approaches to match both the needs and fears of different staff members.

4. Chris would need to reach diverse personality styles within the context of the group, making communicating important information and brainstorming/problem solving more complicated.

5. She would expect varied responses based on how some members usually communicate verbally—or fail to use verbal communication—when asked to share their feelings, thoughts or ideas about an issue.

6. Chris realized again that her first step in getting buy in from her staff was to self evaluate her own responses in the context of her particular combination personality style (a creative, which is a combination of dominant and conscientious).

7. Chris knew her need for control as well as her fear of being criticized could be challenging for her in a system where decisions came "top down", with no input from nursing management. Her own issues with the new CEO included feeling she had no control and that in general he may not even respect her profession.

8. Chris continued to bring her issues to a more experienced mentor. By doing so she could gain emotional support, while also continuing to get wise feedback before initiating any plan of action with her staff.

9. Chris became more proactive, reading books about personality styles to help her view her diverse team as just that—a variety, rather than "good" or "bad" employees.

CHAPTER SIX

Create a Safe Environment— No Bullies Allowed

Just when Chris felt she was becoming more adept at dealing with some leadership issues, Darlene asked to talk with her. Matter-of-factly, Darlene let Chris know she had been offered a nurse manager position at another hospital, and would be leaving in one month. While part of Chris was somewhat relieved, she had come to respect Darlene and her leadership attributes as well.

Chris realized she would miss Darlene's professionalism and shared with the charge nurse that she was sorry to lose her. She also emphasized she valued Darlene's strengths, including her honest communication. Darlene blinked a few times then thanked Chris for acknowledging she was an asset to their facility. Chris then made sure she wished Darlene good luck in her new position, adding that she believed Darlene would be a successful nurse manager. She felt good about how she handled this surprise loss of a team member. Darlene left the facility without any negative behavior being exhibited, at least partially because Chris was so gracious and supportive. Chris even made sure to have a going away party for Darlene, both for all the staff to wish her well and to show she was leaving on good terms with Chris.

Once it sunk in, however, that Chris would have to hire a replacement for Darlene, she felt some trepidation. She had never hired, or for that matter fired, a staff member before. She knew she had to discuss this issue with Marie, as Chris did not want to make a mistake and hire someone who might disrupt her team. However, when she brought up this issue, Marie exhibited what Chris could only describe as a Cheshire Cat smile. Chris gave Marie an inquisitive look. Marie's affect, then became serious and she spoke slowly and deliberately. "Chris," she said, "there is no absolute way to ensure that what you see/hear in an interview is what you will experience once the person is hired and joins your team." Chris was reminded of a line from the movie *Forrest Gump*, (1994) "life is like a box of chocolates, you never know what you are going to get." However, since this choice was so important, Chris didn't think that line sounded as sweet or funny as it had in the movie. This was real life. Nevertheless, Marie had some useful tips to minimize the possibility of accidentally hiring a less than desirable team member. She suggested Chris talk to the Human Resources director and get a list of questions he thought would be important to ask to try to elicit better information about the candidate and help predict how that person might fit within her team. She also encouraged Chris to use some modern interview techniques, asking the candidate how he or she would handle an emergency, for example, or to relate a time the person may have stepped outside policy and procedure. Chris took some time to develop questions she thought would be relevant.

Taking time to prepare for this vital task helped Chris feel at least a little more competent to make a wise decision. The following week she met three candidates who had all been pre-screened by Human Resources and were considered to be viable. She assumed their references were in order. One of the three candidates presented herself as enthusiastic, energetic and friendly. When asked when she had gone outside the parameters of policy and procedure, she answered, "Never." She was also complimentary to Chris. Chris discussed her probable choice with the Human Resources director, who was favorably impressed by her as well. Chris offered the woman the job and she accepted. Although Chris knew she could not be certain this person would become a valued and harmonious member of her team, Brenda seemed to have all the qualifications and attributes of a team-oriented professional. Chris knew, however, as with any new person coming into a system, she would need to wait and see how her new charge RN would fit in.

Brenda arrived on the unit with what Chris perceived as a confident air. She introduced the new charge nurse to both the night and day shifts. Brenda took report from the night shift charge nurse (Deborah), asked a few pertinent questions, and then began making out her assignment immediately. She did not ask any of the staff what patients they usually worked with, so Chris took her aside and let her know a little about the special skills of each of her staff as well as which patients were usually on their assignment. Brenda did not reply, but did adjust the shift assignment in accord with Chris' suggestions. Before Chris left for the morning nursing managers' meeting, however, Brenda asked to see her. Chris was a bit concerned that Brenda might feel she was being controlling by making suggestions regarding matching staff with their usual patients, but Brenda had a different agenda.

Brenda asked Chris if she noticed how dirty the counters were left by the night shift. Chris admitted she did not note any unusual cleanliness issue. Brenda then showed Chris the back portion of the desk, where there was a slight smudge, but not one that most people would notice. Chris started getting that wet feeling on the back of her neck. Would Brenda turn out to be a chronic complainer? She did not want to jump to any conclusions, but did not like the fact that Brenda had only been on the unit less than an hour and already was complaining about another shift. She also knew from experience that even little picky issues between charge nurses could cause, over time, a great deal of unrest and stress between the shifts.

Chris responded to Brenda by acknowledging there was a smudge left on the desk from the night shift, then wiped it off with an antivirus wipe. She did not comment any further, and waited for a response from Brenda. Brenda looked puzzled, but did not pursue the matter any further—that morning. The rest of the shift seemed to run fairly smoothly. Chris hoped Brenda had just had a new employee's need to prove herself, and she would settle down and be less of a perfectionist once she began to fit in with the rest of the team. Unfortunately, that would not be the case.

The next day, again Brenda complained to Chris about the night shift, specifically the night RN, Deborah. She asked Chris to look at the "unfinished admission paperwork" the "lazy night nurse" had left for her to complete. Before Chris responded to the actual complaint, she decided to get more information. She recently had learned that, even though personally she often liked to get "just the facts please", gathering more details she felt she should consider before responding often gave her a more complete picture of an issue. She asked Brenda what time the patient arrived on the unit. Brenda looked taken aback for a moment, and somewhat surprised. However, she looked down at her notes and hesitantly replied that the patient came to the unit at 6:30 a.m. Chris asked if a blood pressure and other vital sign measurements were done. Brenda replied in the affirmative. Chris continued by querying whether a valuables list was completed and the patient was made comfortable on the unit. Again, Brenda had to reply in the affirmative.

Chris then calmly discussed the issue with Brenda, clarifying that what she was saying was part of Brenda's orientation. She pointed out that it was unit policy that, if a patient arrived on the unit later than one hour before the end of a shift, the required parts of the admission were to take vital signs, do a valuable's list and make the patient comfortable. Because all three shifts work as one team, the next shift would pick up the nursing assessment, physician orders and treatment plan parts. Brenda's expression showed she did not look pleased. Chris decided she would not press the matter further at this time, but knew she would have to set some healthy communication norms with Brenda. Chris had never complained about a peer to a supervisor unless the person was truly abusive in some way or performed an act that hurt a patient, and did not herself/himself take responsibility and remedy the error.

Chris felt some trepidation about whether she had made a mistake hiring Brenda. Already she was showing signs that she might create a rift between the shifts. Also, Chris once had been the target of a passive-aggressive peer, now known as one of the types of workplace bullies. Some of her peers had begun treating Chris as if they were mad at her while she had done nothing to deserve that treatment. Even her supervisor at the time had seemed cold to her because the workplace bully was a friend of that nurse manager. Chris had gone to work feeling tense, experiencing both the sweat at the back of her neck and several knots in her stomach on a daily basis. It had gotten so uncomfortable after a while that she had even had stomach pains severe enough for her to stay home from work a few times. Chris had begun to think there was something wrong with her. However, she was lucky—she had a mentor. She had asked the person whether she might be doing something that was making some of her peers and her supervisor treat her as if they did not like or respect her.

Her mentor, who had been researching workplace bullies at that time, had reassured her she was not to blame. In fact her research indicated that most people who are bullied are people who are really good at what they do and have not done anything to hurt the bully. According to *Mobbing, Emotional Abuse in the* Workplace, Davenport, 2005, p.58) . Bullies'*actions may be driven by jealousy and envy derived from feelings of insecurity and fear.* Often the target is one that the bullies feel they can pick on successfully. Chris did a self analysis that day and realized that what was a strength in her own communication style, and in her career achievement, might set her up to be bullied. She was an open, honest communicator, who instinctively trusted other people who seemed nice on the surface. She also was a high achiever, so she understood how some peers might be jealous of her.

Chris decided to preplan what to do with Brenda rather than waiting for her to undermine further and maybe even tear her staff apart by her passive-aggressive behavior. Chris expressed her fears to Marie who nodded solemnly. Marie shared an emotional story of her own about when she had been a new nurse manager. The challenging personality she had faced was a permanent charge nurse on the day shift on her unit. Marie, meanwhile, had been hired from outside the facility. Although the charge nurse initially had smiled and was on the surface friendly with her, Marie had felt uneasy whenever the other nurse was around. While she could not put her finger on exactly what was happening, she had felt it was something, well, just not good.

One day Marie had returned from a nursing leadership meeting and had found the charge nurse facilitating her medication education group. Marie had specifically told her beforehand to ask the patients to just wait a few minutes for her if she were to be late. She had been honest, telling her that this group was her only direct patient care involvement, and that it was so important to her that Marie had negotiated with the DON to be able to lead it when she was hired. She asked the charge nurse what had happened, after letting her complete the group in order not to disturb the patients. The charge nurse had apologized, saying she had misunderstood Marie. Her alleged interpretation was that if Marie were late for the medication group, someone else should start it.

Marie had been about to let the issue go when a patient had approached her looking tense. The patient had shared that she was sad to hear (from the charge nurse) that Marie no longer wanted to lead the group. The patient had continued that this news was upsetting to other patients as well and that some of them had even expressed that they felt rejected by Marie, while others hadn't wanted to "cause any trouble." Marie had thanked the patient and apologized for what she had decided to describe as the "misunderstanding". She then had assured the patient that she was, in fact, fully committed to continuing to facilitate the group. Marie had known she had to confront the charge nurse with what seemed to be an outright lie.

Marie had asked the charge nurse to come into her office, where she could ensure privacy. She had queried the charge nurse for clarification of what had happened, after telling her about the new information she'd received. The charge nurse's face had turned red and she had looked at the floor. Quietly she had admitted she was upset when Marie was hired from outside the facility, because she had also applied for the position and thought the job was hers after what seemed to be a successful interview. At first Marie had sympathized with the charge nurse's disappointment, then had reinforced that she needed each staff member to have open and honest communication with her. She had stressed how the charge nurse's behavior had had a negative impact on the patients, which Marie firmly stated could not be allowed to be repeated.

Although Marie had offered the charge nurse clinical supervision, i.e., another chance, Marie said the other nurse had just stated she would give in her resignation instead. Marie had also made sure to refrain from being negative to the rest of the staff about what the charge nurse had done. She knew two wrongs certainly did not make one right, and she did not want to cause the staff to take sides on the issue. Marie stressed that she believed—partly because she chose to take the "high road" with the charge nurse—that the other nurse had left the facility where she had worked faithfully for over three years, gracefully. She stressed to Chris that whatever Chris felt she needed to do with Brenda when the time came, she would want to maintain what Marie recently learned was called "emotional intelligence" according to Goleman (2004).

Chris just hoped she would not have to experience the same level of undermining behavior from Brenda, or that Brenda would cause an undue amount of stress for the night shift or other staff members. She already felt trepidation about staying in her role, due to what she perceived as the aggressive, cold style of the CEO, along with his tendency to make rapid decisions without consulting with the people who actually did the job, and possibly without considering the ramifications of his decisions. Now she was dealing with a passive-aggressive supervisee. Since it was important to Chris to be able to trust the people she worked with, this type of workplace bully (i.e. the passive-aggressive one that undermines and backbites) was especially difficult for her to attempt to engage positively as a member of her team. On top of it, being the day charge nurse, Brenda also had power over the other staff on the day shift, and was seen as leadership by the other shifts as well. This made her bullying more potentially destructive, because staff tended to respect her position on the team, so she could more easily influence them.

Marie also warned Chris about a new phenomenon called "mobbing" (Davenport 2005), where one bully gets several people to gang up on a vulnerable team member. While Chris did not see Deborah as an "easy mark", due to her ability to stand up for herself assertively, Chris knew that Brenda could make it stressful for her. She also was aware, after talking to Marie, that most people leave their jobs due to having trouble with a peer or boss. Bullying seems to have become a really serious problem in the workplace, and Chris was not about to let a bully rule her unit. She did not have any power to deal with or change the CEO's behavior. However, she did believe that she needed to prevent Brenda from becoming a source of stress that could even result in Chris losing a dedicated and competent night charge nurse or other target Brenda might choose to bully. At this point Chris vowed to at least stop the backbiting to her about Deborah by setting strong norms with Brenda. She would let Brenda know that if she had a problem with another staff member, she needed first to talk to that person face to face. She would teach Brenda, if necessary, how to assertively approach the other person.

Chris also knew that Brenda probably had a long-term issue talking about people rather than directly to them. Sometimes these were family patterns learned in childhood. Often one parent in these homes was someone other family members feared actually confronting to their face. This could include a family where alcohol was a problem, or domestic violence, but not necessarily. The end result, however, was the same. Communication was indirect. Grown up ACOAs (adult children of alcoholics) often have overly high expectations of others, and Chris knew that when a person seems to be "under-adequate," like the alcoholic parent, for example, imperfect perception could also lead the ACOA into being critical of that person.

Chris was aware that she was not a therapist, however, and that doing therapy with her staff was not feasible. In addition, some people who exhibit the bully behavior of backbiting are actually jealous of the target for some reason. She did value Deborah's deep commitment to their patients, her decisiveness in emergencies, etc. but also knew her personality style did not place much value on minor details, like ensuring the back counter was spotless when she left at the end of her shift. Therefore, part of the conflict she perceived between these two charge nurses might also include a conflict in their priorities. Although Chris felt the issue itself was minor, small irritations between the two team leaders could escalate.

Chris thought possibly supplying some education to her team about personality variances and therefore also some priority differences might help as a non-threatening way to start dealing with the issue. She also felt it was important to set the norms for her team, which she knew from past experience needed to include people talking to each other rather than about each other.

Chris discussed both of these ideas with Marie. Marie shared that she was one who valued continuing education, including self and team development as well as clear norms of behavior. She shared that in a book she had recently read, *Primal Leadership* by Daniel Goleman (Goleman 2004), the author strongly recommended creating healthy behavioral norms that the leader both expressed clearly and lived. These norms were one of the ways to develop a healthy team that worked together harmoniously. She said he stressed empathy as an important attribute to have and Chris seemed to have this quality. Chris asked if this meant she could understand the *why* behind someone's behavior, even if she felt the behavior was detrimental, and Marie affirmed this was definitely a part of empathy.

Before actually approaching her staff, therefore, the now more confident nurse manager, decided to spend time working on norms of behavior she knew needed to be embraced in order to keep bullies out of her team. The first thought that came to her mind was "no bullies allowed," because from her own experience and readings, she was aware bullying was the biggest reason that high quality staff left their positions. According to one book she had read, about 80% of bullies were in positions of authority. Again her thoughts drifted to the new CEO. She wondered whether her efforts to develop an effective and harmonious team at her level would be sabotaged by too many cuts in staffing or other administrative decisions that could cause so much increased stress from outside her unit that nothing she could do would be enough.

This being the "monkey in the middle" with no real support from a direct supervisor again made a more daunting project of trying to create a positive atmosphere for people in which to work. However, Chris had never been a quitter. If she did not try to create a healthy microcosm at her workplace, who would?

What did Chris learn about dealing with bullying behavior?

1. Often there may be tension when a qualified person is ready to assume more responsibility, especially when another is promoted "over her." It is best to be gracious and supportive if the person decides to leave on her own. Chris announced Darlene's leaving in a supportive way, and even gave her a going away party.

2. Managers, and not only new managers, can never be sure if the person who interviews well will be an asset or a liability to their team. Using behavioral interviewing, i.e., asking the person how he/she might handle a difficult situation appropriately, sometimes helps determine at least how well the candidate problem solves.

3. If personality testing is not part of a routine for hiring a new team member or leader, a manager can use the techniques already described in this book to get an idea of the interviewee's personality style. However, when people are in an interview situation, they usually put on their best face, and sometimes are savvy enough to give answers they feel the interviewer/potential employer wants to hear, even if that is not their usual way of acting or interacting.

4. Once a new person is hired, there is a period of adjustment to be expected. Some people feel the need to make their mark with the boss. A portion of this group feel if they criticize another person, often a peer, it will make them look better in the eyes of the supervisor. Some people who backbite even use this form of communication as a way to bond with others, including supervisors; i.e., they try to make themselves look better by making another look bad, and in the process create an "us against them" (or her) alliance.

5. Chris was wise enough and had experienced in her past being

the target of a bully, so she was acutely aware of how badly it could affect the target, or even the whole team.

6. She wisely engaged her mentor for advice. She felt validated by Marie's own experience, recognizing that the need to set healthy communication norms was imperative to create a harmonious team.

7. Chris, as did her mentor, continued her education through reading books about leadership issues, specifically the issue of bullying behavior, so she could glean ideas about how to effectively deal with it. For more information about how to handle various types of bullying behavior you can obtain a free report *How to Beat Bully Behavior* at: *www.NurseCareerSuccess. com*.

8. The new nurse manager also did more self assessment and continued to be self aware of bodily cues that let her know her stress level was rising. It was important for her to keep a professional affect and not respond emotionally.

9. Empathy was a concept Chris was familiar with due to caring for patients. It was also an attribute she knew she needed to transfer to difficult situations such as staff conflicts and a potential bully joining her team. By using empathy she could both fully understand what was going on from each staff members point of view and intervene more effectively.

10. Chris was willing to take the time to plan her next step after consulting with her mentor, which was to develop communication norms for her staff. In following chapters Chris will also engage staff as appropriate to help develop norms, etc. as a way to engage the whole team in problem solving. Good leaders know this is also a great way to create buy-in for decisions.

CHAPTER SEVEN

Treat Each Team Member as Valuable

Chris thought long and hard about group norms she wanted the team to both accept and embrace. For one, she knew she wanted people to communicate to each other rather than talk about each other. She especially felt the need to stress how backbiting undermined the team's spirit. She also wanted to introduce cooperation, rather than individual competition, with each team member recognizing the talents and skills of other peers. She knew that to build a strong, healthy team and reduce conflicts, each team member would need to feel valued, both professionally and personally.

Chris made a list of which behaviors she thought would help build a positive team spirit, and reduce the potential for conflict at the same time. However she was not sure setting group norms would help the situation with Brenda, since she assessed Brenda was probably a passive-aggressive type bully. Her hope was that, if the rest of the team bought into building a stellar work group, Brenda might just come along.

She began a draft list of behavioral norms which included:

1. All team members need to talk to each other if they have a disagreement, need to clarify what was said, etc.
2. Team members will use assertive communication; i.e., no blaming or judgmental language. Rather, they should use the assertive format which includes what happened, how the person felt/responded to the incident, and what the person would like to see happen differently the next time.
3. During a team exercise, each team member should identify at

least one skill or positive attribute that is special about every other team member and be able to express how it feels when they are the target of positive feedback rather than negative comments, etc.

4. Backbiting will not be accepted.
5. Sarcastic, demeaning communication will not be accepted.
6. Yelling or other aggressive behavior, of course will not be accepted.

Although Chris did not believe this was a complete list, she did feel good about making a start at developing it. She thought she might present the list to the team to get their input at an all-staff meeting. However, something did not feel right. She discussed what she had accomplished so far with Marie to get her feedback and input. Marie shared that she felt the concept was a good one, and her norms were certainly positive ones to help build a harmonious team. However, she suggested Chris might want to just have a full team meeting with the agenda being to develop group norms. She could bring her list with her in case the team wanted ideas or if they did not volunteer priorities, suggestions, etc. Getting input from the team, Chris realized, would help them have more buy-in to healthy team norms when they were set. Also, the more perspectives and concerns they shared, the more comprehensive could be the teambuilding plan.

Chris decided it would be beneficial to let the staff know in advance about the agenda and recognized that putting a positive emphasis on getting staff to prepare and share could make this a powerful team-building effort in itself. Chris actually felt excited about the prospect of getting her team engaged developing group norms. She also was glad she pre-planned encouraging team input so the group would not just see her as imposing rules on them. This was especially poignant due to the unit staff still trying to positively deal with a staffing cut and the need to badge in rather than sign their time sheets made by the CEO.

Chris thought a two-step process would be beneficial to engage her staff in the process of developing normative behaviors, with a basis of mutual respect. She decided to design a colorful poster, announcing the pre-planning meeting and encouraging the staff to begin a self search of how they wanted their team to treat each other. She would then introduce the importance of shared norms of positive team building behaviors, and clarify with any staff who might not really understand what she was asking of them. She thought using an agenda sheet with space for staff to write notes would be useful for the meeting. Chris always felt more organized when using an agenda, so discussions did not go too far afield or important information was not missed.

Chris was pleased with her idea to make a poster, but also knew art work was not her forte. However, she was aware one of the evening staff members dabbled with art, so she engaged that member to actually create the poster. She was quite pleased with the result, as was the evening staff member. That same PM staff member also committed to being the point person to encourage the evening staff to do self assessment of what was most important to them to create a positive working environment. Chris was glad she asked a staff member for his help, and realized engaging the team as an integral part of the process from the start was a way to empower staff from the inception.

Chris felt enthusiastic when she began the all-staff meeting. However, when she explained what she wanted the staff to co-create, some of the quieter team members looked puzzled. She was not sure if she had been unclear, but remembering she was dealing with different personality styles, Chris chose to use a variety of ways to explain group communication and behavioral norms. She noted the quiet ones nodding their heads after the expanded explanation, while admittedly some of the staff looked a little bored, as they were the personality type that wants "just the facts." Once she finished introducing the concept, however, several people chimed in with what they felt were the most important behaviors a team needed to exhibit to work well together. Many of the staff identified indirect communication as being a real problem. When asked what that meant to these people, they could identify several indirect communication behaviors. These included:

1. Talking negatively about people behind their backs while pretending to be friends to their faces, and engaging others to create an "us against them" or against him/her atmosphere.
2. Making sarcastic remarks.
3. Rolling their eyes and sighing, rather than saying what they feel.
4. Saying they will do something, then not doing it.
5. Blaming others for their feelings, but couched in a way that instills guilt.

6. Using a condescending tone when talking to people with whom they may have issues.
7. Not speaking to people when they are upset.
8. Wearing a surface smile while talking "through their teeth" when they are upset.

When Chris asked about any overt aggressive behaviors, she was heartened to hear that none of the staff from any of the shifts were experiencing overt yelling, name calling or threats. She gave the staff immediate positive feedback on their maturity and stressed that this group of people was already more advanced in building a stellar team working environment than most. Ida then stifled a cough and looked uncomfortable. Chris acknowledged her discomfort and encouraged her to share what she was thinking. The usually garrulous evening charge nurse spoke almost in a whisper.

She admitted she had been recently yelled at by one of the new doctors when she asked him to clarify a phone order. While this action had occurred on the telephone—and Ida quickly added that she knew the doctor was technically not part of their team—she admitted she had felt belittled and upset. She stated he had also said she "must be stupid or something" when, not sure if she had heard the order clearly, she asked him to spell the name of a medication he was prescribing. The nurse then quickly added she did not want to say anything negative about the doctor "behind his back" and that she knew she should have "thicker skin" by now, after working with physicians for years. However, since the rest of the physicians who had been with the hospital a longer time seemed to work so well with their nurse colleagues, this new doctor's behavior had taken her by surprise.

While Chris admitted the staff did not have any control over physicians' behavior, she did recommend that once the staff created their microcosmic healthy environment, they might begin to influence the hospital in general. Chris did express concern about the new physician's behavior and stated she would let nursing management know there may be a problem with nurse bullying by this doctor, which could not be tolerated in a modern facility. Ida became anxious, and expressed she was afraid of repercussions from this new doctor, so the team decided to implement a two nurse telephone order rule to protect them; i.e., two nurses would let the physician know they were on the telephone line together to ensure accuracy of taking the verbal order. The physician would get the point quickly that if he exhibited grossly overt inappropriate behavior such as yelling and name calling, there would be two professionals listening, one being a witness for the other.

Chris clarified this was not indirect communication, but rather an affective self defense behavior she had learned early in her career. She shared an incident that had involved a new nurse and a chronically haughty doctor, who had been called at night for new orders. The doctor had had a distinct Middle Eastern accent and had responded appropriately to the nurse who used his name when she called. However, the next day, he had denied ever having given the orders. Luckily, administration had not overreacted, since the orders had been sound and fit the diagnosis of the patient. That is when nursing administration had instituted the two nurse verbal telephone order rule with this doctor. Ida shared that she felt more comfortable with this action. Chris also clarified that while doctors were not technically part of their team, and therefore could not be part of the group developing norms that would help create a healthy working environment, how doctors interface with them certainly was an important factor in determining job satisfaction for the professional nursing staff.

Chris noted, after making this self-protective plan, that the nurses smiled and nodded, seeming to feel more empowered. The team then set out to take the behaviors they were not pleased had occurred within their group, and create proactive statements from them. This is the first draft the team formulated:

1. We promise to talk to each other when we are upset, rather than about anyone else, and will only engage other people when we want to compliment a peer; i.e., there is only "us."
2. We promise to think before we say something, then do so calmly and respectfully.
3. We promise to be aware of our non-verbal habits, such as rolling our eyes if we have something to say, and instead say it.
4. We promise to take responsibility for our own actions.
5. We promise to do what we say we will do, and say no if we can't do it.
6. We promise to be more aware of our feelings, and if we feel angry, take a moment before talking to someone to avoid sounding condescending.

7. We promise to use our voice and speak up when we disagree with someone, to avoid isolating ourselves through silence.
8. We promise to be in touch with any incongruent behavior, such as smiling but talking between clenched teeth, to avoid insincere communication which is confusing to others.

While Chris knew these beginning statements which her staff chose to write as promises or commitments were only a rough draft, she was impressed by their self awareness.

The now not-so-new nurse manager complimented the staff members on their accomplishment and their commitment to making their unit an even better place to work. She noted several smiles from the staff and a buzz of discussion as they left the meeting. She felt really good about her job that day. Maybe middle management was not as bad as she had originally thought.

Chris enthusiastically shared the staff's first draft of healthy communication/behavioral norms with Marie that evening. Marie smiled and her affect seemed to Chris to be almost as happy as she felt. While Chris knew creating a healthy work environment was only one way to value each and every one of her staff members, she did feel this was an important first step.

Chris then shared some creative ways she had learned from other nursing leaders to help the staff recognize each other. For example, a DON from a small nursing home initiated the "quarter system." Every staff member at the facility brought at least one quarter with them to their work stations. Then when someone did something a staff member recognized was especially thoughtful or nice, that person would smile and hand the other staff member a quarter. Her staff seemed to have fun with this peer recognition. Marie thought this was a creative idea for staff to both recognize each other and add a little fun to the day as well.

Chris committed to herself to continue increasing her own EI (emotional intelligence), as she knew she had high expectations of herself and others and wanted to make sure she came across respectfully to all staff members. She further committed to utilize her new knowledge of differences of staff's recognition needs, so she would not just use a "cookie cutter" approach that would only be effective with a portion of the staff. This management thing was complicated to say the least, but Chris felt she was getting a handle on it.

While she also knew some people who interfaced with the team might not be committed to the same respect level she wanted to see from the nursing staff, i.e., the one physician, she felt positive that she could be creative in at least helping to protect the nurses from his verbal assaults. After doing some research, Chris felt blessed that only one new doctor was exhibiting this nurse bullying behavior, as she heard it was still fairly common in some other facilities.

While Chris was the object of an occasional sharp or sarcastic remark from physicians in the past, none had ever called her "stupid." Later that evening, she did some self awareness work and found herself almost obsessing about how upset she felt over the physician's disrespect for her professional colleague. Suddenly, Chris remembered being yelled at by a teacher in elementary school because she had not put her pencil down fast enough at the end of a test period. While the teacher hadn't exactly call her stupid, his tone had been harsh and his look said to her she had really done something awful. She had felt shame at that time, and had almost cried. It hit her that her colleague may have felt shamed by the doctor's words, much like Chris had felt from her childhood teacher's tone and stern, criticizing look.

While she did not feel she needed to share this insight with Ida, Chris did realize how destructive overt hostile behavior was to a healthy work environment. After all, even though we all grow up, each of us still feel shame or other negative emotions such as fear, which Ida shared when Chris suggested someone in authority might need to become aware of the new physician's behavior to head off future "attacks". Chris thought dealing with diverse people really was a challenge, especially when some of them seemed either to be unaware of how their behavior affected others, or worse—as in the case of the new doctor—to not even care.

Chris was happy with the initial team effort at developing group communications/behavioral norms. Being aware of clear team expectations could help new people like Brenda both fit in and become bonded with people she would be spending many of her waking hours with, if she chose to be part of the group. Setting clear boundaries of acceptable behavior could facilitate building a cohesive team by helping people from different backgrounds find common ground. She was not sure whether Brenda would be a good fit for the team. However, by setting healthy team expectations, Brenda just might become frustrated and leave of her own accord. Bullies, Chris knew from reading about this vital current topic, account for more staff stress and turnover than almost any other work environment issue. What she could do about the new doctor, however, was a different story. She had no authority over him, and when it came to "taking sides" in a hospital setting, the upper administration seemed to favor the more powerful and valued professional, which of course is a doctor.

What did Chris learn about building a cohesive team, and healthy work environment?

1. Each team member needs to feel valued, recognized and accepted.
2. To reduce conflict, it is important to stress the need for cooperation, rather than competition, within the team.
3. Creating a list of communication/behavioral norms is one way to clearly state expectations for team members.
4. To get maximum buy-in, using a democratic leadership style usually works well. Chris encouraged staff input identifying behaviors they felt were needed to create harmony and mutual respect within the team. That input also reflected each team member's values.
5. Once group norms are agreed upon, it is important to remind staff it is each member's responsibility to ensure they are followed, not just the leader's job.
6. Make sure new employees are made aware of these behavioral expectations during their orientation, because if people are not informed of what is and what is not acceptable behavior, they will often act as they have habitually done in the past.
7. Sometimes a few staff members are unable, or unwilling, to change their behavior. These people often exclude themselves from a team that is passionately committed to healthy, respectful behavior, especially if they are caught in untruths, as is often the case with the passive-aggressive bully.

CHAPTER EIGHT

Trouble Shoot Continually

Chris began to feel more comfortable in her role after helping her staff create healthy norms of behavior and doing her own self assessment—again. She was aware, however, that there is always a "honeymoon" phase when a positive change occurs. Even though she could see how enthusiastically some of the team seemed to embrace wanting to create a respectful, cohesive environment, stressing team cooperation rather than competition, she also knew actually getting people to live these norms would be a longer term process. She reminded herself again of the nursing process: assessment (with diagnosis of problems), planning, implementation and evaluation. Now that the team was beginning to implement their shared list of behaviors, Chris would need to continually evaluate how well they were actually being followed.

She decided to include the staff in this process as well, asking them at each all-staff meeting how they felt the new norms for behavior were working. She would then ask for some ways to improve the process if people felt that some of the staff was only giving lip service to the norms, without pointing a finger at any one person in particular. This would be a delicate process because she knew asking for feedback of this kind often could result in a personal attack on one or another staff member. She wanted to create a balance in the team, holding each member accountable for his or her behavior while not singling anyone out as a "bad guy."

Chris talked to Marie about how best to approach the staff in order to keep the feedback general enough so it did not come across as being critical of one or more staff members, because she knew that different personality styles needed more time to adjust to any change. Even though most of these staff members tended to be quieter than the few more outspoken people, they could also be the ones who talked more *about* another person instead of *to* the other person, for fear of retaliation from the stronger personality styles. She had to maintain that safe environment of "no bullies allowed," while simultaneously discouraging an attack on the people who might exhibit bullying behavior.

Marie acknowledged Chris' dilemma, and suggested she stay neutral, especially in a first meeting, asking for feedback about implementing the new norms. She explained if Chris just asked the staff to rate how well they felt the team was doing in creating an assertive, respectful work environment while refraining from giving specific examples, it might give Chris valuable information without the threat of making someone a scapegoat. Sometimes people are actually struggling to fit in with the group, but due to their individual backgrounds and lack of self awareness, may not be changing quickly enough for some of the other group members. Chris thought this was a good idea.

During the next all-staff meeting Chris smiled, and asked the staff to rate, on a scale of one to ten, how respected they felt before the norms were implemented, and how they felt now that they were newly implemented. Chris said she would ask this question each month during the all-staff meeting, to get an idea of the subjective effectiveness of the new norms. The staff seemed to respond well to this exercise, some smiling, others looking thoughtful and nodding. Only Brenda seemed to look puzzled. Chris now had another *aha* moment. Brenda did not seem to even comprehend the importance of respectful, open communication and other positive behaviors. She realized Brenda probably did not know what healthy behavior was, nor that she was in fact trying to undermine her or "wreak havoc" on the team with her passive aggressive criticisms. She just plain did not seem to know any better.

With this new insight into Brenda's communication challenges, Chris chose a different path to attempt to coach her. She would invite Brenda to help her with a project, in which Brenda would need to communicate directly with Chris on an ongoing basis. The nurse manager felt this would be a good way to build rapport with Brenda, which might help the adverse behavior to cease of its own accord. From her research Chris knew that people who felt connected, as well as valued as individuals, usually were less likely to need to draw attention to themselves by criticizing others. Chris was not sure what project she could enlist Brenda's help in, as being the charge nurse on the day shift did not leave much time for any extra activity. Chris brainstormed with Marie to come up with an idea to engage Brenda without overloading her with work. They both shared ideas, then Marie got what appeared to Chris to be a twinkle in her eye. She suggested having Brenda start the quarter system "chain" each day; i.e., it would be Brenda's duty to "catch" someone doing something special for a patient, staff member or visitor. She would then be expected to smile and hand the person a quarter.

Chris was not sure if this tactic would work with Brenda, but she was willing to give it a try. Surprisingly when she asked Brenda, as the new charge nurse, to start the chain of positive feedback on the day shift, Brenda smiled. She appeared to feel that Chris thought she was special and was acknowledging her leadership role on her shift. Although Chris knew this was not necessarily an indicator of success, the nurse manager began to see a more positive side of Brenda. It might be that Brenda could become a valuable asset to the team, rather than a thorn in Chris' side.

Although she also knew that using a creative management technique learned from another successful leader provided no guarantee, it gave Chris more incentive to think outside the box. She would, however, need to keep an eye on Brenda's behavior for a time to ensure she was beginning to engage in a positive manner with the rest of the team, including the night charge nurse. Often just being keenly aware of non-verbal communication could help in this ongoing assessment process. She would make sure to watch, not just listen to, interactions between the two charge nurses. She was getting better at picking up subtle cues that might indicate some stress between the two strong personalities, even if they kept a civil tone, and the content of their conversations were not overtly hostile, sarcastic, etc.

Being a person and thus a leader who liked to finish one project then move forward to another one, Chris knew she had to remember being a leader of a human "open system" such as a unit meant that nothing really stayed the same. Therefore, she would have to continually assess the tone of the unit, staff interaction, and herself in order to effectively respond to changes and adapt to them in a positive manner. Her nursing education, she realized, did help her prepare for dealing not only with various personalities, a four-generation workforce and different communication styles, but also the complexity of the interactions between the various people. At that moment, it felt less like Brenda was an outsider who might not fit in. Rather, she might be a person who was reacting to someone who she perceived to be a threat. That person could either be someone very unlike her, or in the case of the night charge nurse, may be too much like her. Two strong personalities often tended to overly compete with each other to be the "best," or at least be the most respected or liked by people in authority.

Leading this diverse group would be an ongoing challenge for the nurse manager, but it also seemed to be one she felt could help her stretch to her full potential as a leader. Chris never really liked easy jobs, and being a nursing middle manager surely was <u>not</u> an easy job. However, Chris was feeling more solid in her position, and with Marie's ongoing mentoring she felt more confident she would continue to succeed. She wished she knew what the upper management had planned for the rest of her first year, however, as each change that needed to be implemented would cause more stress, especially when the changes came suddenly, without warning or time to prepare the staff for them.

Chris could admit to herself, however, that some things were out of her control. She did not like this realization, being a responsible person of action, but knew it was true. Ongoing assessment, therefore had to include being prepared to deal with the unexpected, maybe even on a daily basis. Although this seemed like a daunting expectation, Chris was feeling more positive that she was up for the challenge.

What did Chris learn about the continuous need for trouble shooting?

1. In order to succeed in a middle management position, it is necessary to be constantly vigilant, especially during the "honeymoon" phase of a change, because staff may be slow to demonstrate emotional reactions and it takes time for many people to change.
2. Include staff, using a democratic leadership style whenever possible, especially when you want to get maximum buy-in which will result in true change, not just lip service.
3. It is wise to engage a positive mentor or leadership coach to brainstorm new ideas before implementing them.

4. Take your time when trying to make a major shift, such as creating and implementing group behavioral norms. This change may be major for some people, depending on their personal value systems.

5. Make an effort to come across in a pro-active way. Be aware some staff members may have used a passive aggressive communication style, for example, a good portion of their lives, or at least in their careers. It is wise, therefore, to try to find a way to communicate the positives of assertive communication without sounding critical.

6. Bullies in the workplace are now the number one reason people leave jobs, even ones they otherwise like very much. It is therefore important to be constantly vigilant to discover and quickly deal with bullying behavior before it escalates.

7. Engaging a person who appears to exhibit bullying behavior creatively may give the person the positive attention she (or he) needs. Chris put Brenda in charge of the quarter system chain to help Brenda both embrace and practice a team building activity. This creative approach replaced the need to set limits on the behavior she exhibited against the night charge nurse, which had the potential to tear their team apart.

8. Chris also knew Brenda's response would depend on Brenda, and she was aware she would need to monitor this staff member more closely than others for some time before she could trust that Brenda would not slip back into her old ways.

9. Chris also learned to go deeper in self assessment, and remember she was the leader of an "open system, " where nothing really would stay the same. Thus she would need to help the team adapt continually.

10. Difficult to swallow, but true—some things are out of a middle manager's control. Therefore Chris also learned she might just need to help her staff adjust to new decisions, that she had little or no input into being made.

CHAPTER NINE

Enjoy the Process

Chris reassessed how she felt about her position. Middle management was just that, the person in the middle. She already accepted that she was leading not one but actually three teams, with somewhat diverse priorities. The day shift had to ensure lab tests were completed by lab personnel, and took care of the majority of discharges for patients. The evening shift dealt with the majority of admissions and the night shift was responsible for the majority of the paperwork. Each shift also seemed to have a slightly different group personality due to the various individual personalities coming together. However, Chris was also part of the nursing management and full management teams. While they overlapped, there was a difference in the feeling of each of the meetings, with the full management meeting being the one where Chris felt the most tension.

Chris, therefore, could only be the leader on her unit, although she felt she might have some impact on the nursing management group. The DON did encourage open communication and discussion about issues over which she had authority. Therefore, Chris decided she would attempt to stay as positive and proactive as possible when meeting with this group, while realizing there were boundaries and limits as to how much impact that team might have within the organization. To be more proactive, she looked into Plane Tree, a country-wide system that helped create a caring atmosphere that could facilitate patients returning to health more quickly. She also explored how hospitals could get Magnet status. Both of these programs stressed excellence of patient care, and if Magnet status was achieved, the hospital could attract really motivated, pro-active and professional nurses to come to work there.

Thinking about ways to empower nurses to be able to develop beyond her initial hopes of group healthy behaviors and introducing positive creative actions, such as the quarter system, helped Chris feel even more enthusiastic about her job. She asked Marie what she thought could be other ways to help her staff deal with day-to-day stress and enjoy their jobs more. Marie asked Chris how her own stress level was doing. Although Chris wanted to answer the traditional "just fine," she knew she did take life too seriously sometimes. In fact, she knew she was a real worrier. She worried about a lot of what-ifs, such as, *What if the CEO were to make another demand on the nursing staff that could affect both their collective self esteem and ability to perform excellent patient care?* and, *What if Brenda decided to revert back to her passive aggressive behavior, and go even deeper underground with it?*

Worrying had been one of Chris' stressors since childhood. Although she learned many positive values and healthy behaviors from her mother and generally felt a positive sense of her own self worth, she also learned the worry habit from the same source. Chris smiled when she recalled an incident where she encouraged her mother to try not to worry about something bad that might happen. Unfortunately that time, something adverse did occur. Her mother admonished her saying, "I told you what would happen if we just left it up to chance." It startled Chris to realize her mother actually felt empowered through worry, that somehow if you worried enough, whatever you were worrying about would turn out all right.

Worrying was so automatic with Chris that she caught a reflection of her face in a window while she was busily engaged full throttle in this behavior, and was stunned to see a deep furrow in her brow while she was contemplating how to get the staff enthused about the quarter system!

When Chris asked herself why presenting a concept so positive could give her so much trepidation, the answer surprised her. Her answer was, "I am afraid people might laugh at me for introducing such a fun activity." That is when Chris decided she was just plain taking her role too seriously, as she had done many times in the past. Change can be fun, she told herself, even though the principle behind the fun activity is seriously important. This self assessment was a real eye opener for Chris. Being part

D in personality, she really wanted her team, as well as herself, to succeed. However, getting to the finish line in the race for superior patient care, she identified, did not need to feel like she was running a twenty-six mile marathon! Chris smiled as she imagined herself sweating, panting and nearly passing out trying to accomplish that feat.

She made a conscious choice that day to enjoy coming to work every morning. She was not sure exactly how to get into this frame of mind, but was determined to come in with a smile, and focus on at least one positive thing. Chris realized this mindset change could be as simple as consciously appreciating that her car was running well or maybe acknowledging the night shift's usual thoughtfulness for making a pot of coffee for the day shift. Chris knew if she did not focus on something positive, it was easy to concentrate on all the problems that might come up that day. Yes, that pesky "worry wart" could easily rear its ugly head at any time, she thought. Chris made up her mind that she would no longer succumb to that old family belief. She knew it would not be easy, since she had been a worrier for, well, most of her life, just like her mother. However, once Chris made up her mind to change something, she knew she was just stubborn enough to do it. She then laughed at herself, because of course when she felt compelled to do something she usually did so with the proverbial stiff upper lip attitude. That was exactly the opposite of how she wanted to come across with her staff.

Chris decided she needed to discuss how she could lighten up and still be taken seriously as a leader by the staff as well as her supervisors, so she asked her mentor. Marie looked pensive for a moment, then asked Chris to describe a good and effective leader. Chris pondered for a few seconds, then she described her favorite supervisors. She shared they were people who seemed to genuinely care about the staff, as people as well as professionals. That is, they gave quick positive feedback for any extra effort made by a staff member, smiled warmly when they greeted each person, and made good eye contact. They also had a sense of humor, and could somehow make either drudge work or stressful situations seem less daunting. She could not describe exactly what they did to create a more calm and positive state on the unit, but they just seemed to be able to do it. Marie asked Chris what she did to help herself stay calm in stressful situations. Chris did not have an answer, and she felt as if she would need to take more time for some self assessment on that issue.

After several minutes of contemplating how she managed her own stress, Chris did identify that if she remembered to take several deep breaths, it seemed to clear her head and help her better problem solve. She wondered whether others would notice if she used this simple technique and become more focused and less stressed as well. She decided to try it the next day, along with coming in with a smile and greeting each staff member by name and with good eye contact. She would also look for little "extras" so she could give staff positive feedback.

It was easier than she thought to actually remember to smile, etc. as soon as she reached the unit. Chris was surprised at how much more positive she felt when she smiled and acknowledged each staff member as a person to start her day. What was a pleasant unexpected bonus for herself, however, was the response from the other staff. Except for Brenda, of course, everyone smiled back at her. She could actually feel the positive energy in the room. That is when Chris really got it and did not succumb to her own usual driven-for-perfection style. She understood she could either help create an upbeat and positive ambience on the unit, or an uptight and anxious one, because as a leader staff would take their cue for behavior from her. That whole shift seemed to go by quickly and with less problems. Of course, the staff worked hard to keep up with all the patients' needs, on a fast-paced hospital floor. However, somehow it didn't feel quite so serious.

When Chris decided to bring this positive attitude into the weekly nursing management meeting, she was not sure how much impact she could make. In this team she was a peer with one supervisor, the DON. She wondered if only one person could influence the usual somber tone of the meeting, or if she would be considered as odd or out of touch with the rest of this group if she tried this new behavior. Chris decided it was worth the risk, because up to this time she had felt anxious whenever she thought about attending it. Being too serious, it seemed was an affliction of the entire nursing management team. Although she could feel the sweat starting at the back of her neck when she entered the room, she resolved, but not too intensely, to smile and try to lighten up the meeting. Luckily she was prepared for the bewildered look on her fellow nurse managers' faces when she entered the room with a smile, while their faces showed the usual frozen serious, tense look.

The DON was the first to ask Chris why she seemed to be so happy that day, when the department so recently was short-staffed and professionals were still expressing hurt feelings over having to punch a time clock. Chris paused a second or two, took one of her deep breaths, then answered in a calm voice. She acknowledged that the department was still struggling to accommodate these two changes, but added that she was trying on her own unit to put the focus on what her staff was doing to both continue to give excellent patient care and build each other up as team members. She explained how recently she had instituted the quarter system, for example, and how much the staff seemed to enjoy it. She also shared how she had noticed that when she modified her usual very serious nature, it seemed to help her staff feel calmer and create a more positive atmosphere for the patients as well.

Chris thought the DON looked a bit startled at first, but then a smile crept across her face. She asked the other nurse managers if they felt she might be too serious at times. Chris nodded and so did most of the other leadership people. The DON then asked what would she need to do, and this group need to do, to help feel more focused and less stressed. Several leaders shared what they felt would help, including focusing more on the things they could control. Some noted they felt trying out the quarter system or some other immediate reward system could be helpful with their staff. The DON added she wanted something special for this team as well. Although they could not directly change what occurred from above, they did have the power to create a more healthy, pro-active team both within the leadership group and extending to each nurse manager's unit. Chris had never seen the DON so animated before. She, like Chris, tended to be serious in nature. She liked this new boss much better.

Chris realized that just one person could affect the mood of not just a whole unit, where that person was the designated leadership person, but also a peer group, and even a supervisor. That realization empowered Chris to continue to try new ways to enjoy her job personally and share this feeling with her staff. She even shared her enthusiasm with her husband, who chuckled. He then admitted that while he loved her passion for her work, it was refreshing to hear she would try not to take it so seriously. Chris almost started to clarify that she meant she was just trying to lighten up her mood, etc., but caught herself. She told herself her loving husband was not making fun of her, or disrespecting her professionalism. He was just sharing his opinion that in fact she sometimes took her job, and probably life in general, too seriously.

Chris decided that in order to maintain enthusiasm at her job, she needed to "fill herself up" physically, emotionally and spiritually outside of work. While Chris was not too religious, she and her husband did attend a modern church, and enjoyed hanging out with other like-minded people for coffee or their monthly church dinner. They decided as a couple, however, to add a gratefulness prayer at night, reflecting on what was going right for their family, etc. She had also read about meditation, and how it actually thickened the frontal lobe of the brain. She could use this extra help to stay calm under sometimes even emergency situations. She liked deep breathing and one book had said a simple meditation could just be to become aware of her breath while she tried to breathe slowly and deeply. This technique was one she would attempt first, although she liked several others she explored as well. She decided to start with only about five minutes per day, but wanted to extend this practice to at least twenty minutes, when she could better quiet her thoughts. Chris found her worry thoughts liked to creep in the most, followed by her list of things she had to finish that day. Becoming aware of these pesky distractions, Chris vowed, would not deter her from continuing her practice. After all, one book said that we western hemisphere people have the most trouble of all becoming quiet enough to listen to our inner wisdom.

Chris also decided to make it a point to take a walk outside in good weather, swim at the local pool, or ride her stationery bicycle at least every other day. She knew from her nursing background that just twenty minutes to one half hour every other day could make a difference in how well she managed daily stress. She also knew that aerobic exercise would increase her energy and mood. Thinking about actually doing the exercise as she knew she "should" however, would be more challenging. Then Chris remembered one of her friends had recently asked her to go swimming. She decided to ask that friend if she would be her exercise buddy. That way each friend could encourage the other when one just plain did not feel like exercising. She was pretty sure her chosen "buddy" would be happy to have someone there for her when she needed motivation and Chris could depend on her support as well. She decided to call her friend that day.

Chris knew she felt more energetic and happier when she made a point of planning at least one fun activity per week with her husband and also took some "alone time". Both she and her husband liked to eat at ethnic restaurants, and enjoyed adventure movies on the big screen. They chose restaurants often with softer lighting and that were not too crowded so they could recapture some of the romance of their dating years. Chris also loved when her husband put his arm around her at the movies. It made her feel like a teenager again to just cuddle with him, although sharing a bag of popcorn was also fun. She smiled just thinking about spending a romantic evening with him. Since they did not have children, it of course was easier to get away. However, friends of Chris had baby sitters they trusted with their children so they, too, could have some special "couples" time alone.

Chris loved nature, so when she planned to take her alone time, she usually took a ride down a scenic road or a walk in the park by the river near her home. She loved both trees and water, and seemed to feel more connected when she was out in nature. Just imagining being in her favorite walking area brought a smile to her face and she found herself taking a slow, deep, satisfying breath. Despite being a high energy person naturally, Chris knew she needed to take time to fill up her energy tank, just as she did to make sure her car was filled with high quality gas in order for it to run at peak performance.

In addition, to help be at her best, Chris knew from her nursing background she needed to plan her meals to include those five servings of fruit/vegetables in her diet. She knew chocolate, which at times of stress seemed to be a food group in itself, would need to be relegated to more of an occasional treat—darn it. Emotional eating had been an issue for Chris since she was a child. She could remember her mother saying that if she received a good grade on a test, for example, she would make Chris a batch of fudge to celebrate. Whenever Chris visited her mother, even to this day, almost the first words that came out of her mom's mouth were, "What would you like to eat?" Chris realized the act of feeding people was a family value which seemed to be a way to show love. Was it any wonder she was a few pounds overweight? If food was synonymous with love, then when Chris felt stressed, it made sense to her that she would snack when she was alone, or in a situation where she could not ask her husband for a hug.

Chris took a deep breath. All this self assessing was exhausting at times. However, she vowed she would begin writing out a list of small changes she could accomplish to help feel more energetic and happy, so she could better deal with daily stress at work. She remembered reading how daily journaling was also a good way to identify any current issues that might be causing her more stress in her life as well as feelings she might have that were just below the surface of her consciousness. One author, Chris remembered, suggested writing anything that came to mind in a free flowing manner first thing in the morning, before the busy thoughts began deluging her brain. Chris felt a little queasy about starting this practice, however, since she was not sure what might come out. She also was a little wary that someone else might see what she wrote, like her husband. When she realized this was her fear, Chris questioned herself why it would matter to her if he did read her journal. Again, the answer was that, despite the fact they had been happily married for five years and he was continually supportive to her, there was still that little voice inside that warned Chris he might think some of what she wrote would be laughable.

Chris knew she was not an especially articulate writer, except for her nursing notes, which were clear, detailed and accurate. Chris had to tell herself that journaling was not professional writing. She reminded herself she was not going to expect her journal to be published or win a Pulitzer prize or anything! The entries would be just her own thoughts, feelings, and wants. She then asked herself, when had she ever felt her husband would snoop if she asked him not to, and for that matter, when had he laughed at her endeavors? The answer, to her satisfaction was, never that she could remember. In fact, most often Chris shared her innermost feelings, thoughts and desires with him anyway. Feeling more confident, Chris decided to buy a special book in which to journal, one with colors and maybe an upbeat picture.

Chris smiled to herself, as she usually was conservative in her dress and the way she decorated both her home and office. She thought that conservative gave off a more professional air, at least at work. However, in order to lighten up, she decided to put a picture of herself and her husband, taken on their last vacation—to Hawaii, complete with bright patterned shirts and flower necklaces—right in the middle of her desk. That way she would be sure to start her day by gazing at a representation of a happy time shared with her best friend and life partner. This lightening up stuff was beginning to become more fun for her. She hoped her new more positive attitude would be contagious to the rest of her staff.

What did Chris learn about enjoying work and life more?

1. Middle management is really being the leader "in the middle." In some leadership groups she had little or no input into management decisions being made.

2. Some leaders' personalities (especially those like Chris with her high D), take the need to succeed too seriously.

3. Consciously enjoying the day could help decrease stress in both the leader and her team(s).

4. Self assessment led to Chris identifying herself as a worry wart, and she realized focusing on the what-ifs would both rob her of needed energy and make it more difficult to focus on current issues, over which she might have more control.

5. Chris identified her worrying behavior as being learned in childhood from her mother. Early beliefs such as this one can be more challenging to change, because they have been so engrained and automatic for so many years.

6. When she was compelled to do something, Chris often approached the task with the proverbial stiff upper lip. However, often lightening up a stressful situation can make the task more palatable, maybe even a bit fun.

7. Chris made a conscious choice to greet each staff member with a smile, give immediate positive feedback for extra effort that she witnessed and make good eye contact. She would bring this positive attitude into management meetings as well.

8. Since she had a sense of humor, Chris vowed to interject it, especially when there was a lot of drudge work to do, such as mounds of paperwork.

9. She wanted also to keep a certain level of calm on the unit, and realized she needed to maintain a peaceful, positive attitude in order to help create this ambiance.

10. In nursing management meetings she suggested they try to focus more on things they could control, rather than on the two decisions recently made by the new CEO, to help create a more pro-active team. She realized that just one positive person could also influence peers, and maybe even a direct supervisor, not just staff she led.

11. In order for her to deal more effectively with her own stress, Chris decided to utilize several stress management techniques:

    a. Say a gratefulness prayer before bed (with her husband) to focus on what was going well in their lives.

b. Spend a few minutes every morning breathing slowly and deeply and explore other simple forms of meditation.

c. Spend a minimum of twenty minutes to one half hour at least every other day doing an enjoyable aerobic exercise. Engage an exercise buddy to help stay motivated and enjoy the process more.

d. Plan at least one fun activity per week with her husband and also take some alone time.

e. Pre-plan meals to include the basic food groups, even though chocolate often seemed to Chris to be a member of all of the food groups, depending on the day.

f. Write in her journal her feelings, ideas, wants every morning—about three free-flowing pages—to help her get more in touch with her inner self and problem solve more creatively. Chris learned to laugh a bit at her high expectations, because she knew she was not a professional writer and journaling is free writing that sometimes contained poor grammar or misspellings!

12. In order to enjoy her job more, Chris had to start dealing more effectively with her own stress, but found the process energizing and it helped her increase her enthusiasm for her job. She needed to be "filled up" emotionally/spiritually and fuel her body well before she could expect to create a more stress-free environment at work.

(Go to *www.NurseCareerSuccess.com* for more stress management tips.)

CHAPTER TEN

Achieve a Team Spirit (Cooperation, not Competition)

Once Chris decided to enjoy the process of leading her teams and being part of the nursing management team as well as a member of the full management team, she asked herself what would be her next step in her leadership development. She pondered this question for some time, then another *aha* moment occurred when she least expected it. Chris was in a nursing management meeting, and while awaiting the arrival of the DON, she listened to one of her peers lamenting. The other nurse manager shared she was having trouble getting the three shifts to work and think as if they were part of the same team. The day shift basically came across in one of her all-staff meetings as being the "all important" shift. The evening shift seemed to fight back with their belief they worked harder than any other shift, due to having to admit the most patients. The night shift shared a feeling of being slighted and unappreciated while they anchored the team by ensuring the paperwork was completed, charts were readied for the next day, etc.

The fellow nurse manager said the tension in the room during her last all-shift meeting was awful. The three shifts seemed to be angry with each other. She was astute enough to identify that this rift seemed to be more obvious after the recent changes from the CEO, so she at first attributed it to misdirected anger toward other shifts. Chris nodded, saying that she felt this could be a contributing factor. However, both she and the other nurse managers agreed that this type of shift competition was not healthy.

They decided to discuss ways each of them could help their shifts feel more valued and their unique contributions acknowledged. They realized, as a leadership group, that unhealthy competition could occur between two staff members or between shifts and that developing a team spirit would be beneficial. However, the group became quiet at that point. How could they change a belief from shift or individual competition to group cooperation? Chris did not have any ready answers, but she was glad the other nurse manager brought up the issue. She felt some of Brenda's backbiting had to do with a basic belief that in order for her to win—i.e., be considered an important valued professional—she had to make someone else, such as her peer the night charge nurse, look bad.

Chris wondered if it was not just a personality style difference rather than a learned bully behavior that motivated Brenda. Maybe she felt—at least partially—as if she were undervalued, or was less popular than the night charge RN, whom most of the staff liked. She shared this observation with the rest of the nurse manager team, who agreed they all were experiencing at least a couple of staff members who might not believe in the concept of cooperation, not just the one nurse manager who experienced shift against shift competition. They began to brainstorm how they could encourage people to work more harmoniously together. The leadership group decided they needed ways to help develop more team spirit. The quarter system was one way Chris utilized that seemed to work to at least help on a grass roots level to have one staff member at a time acknowledge the extra effort of another. While this simple technique only validated one person at a time and could also end up being misused or overused by someone trying to manipulate his/her peers into liking the giver more, it was one way to get people to focus on someone else's "greatness" rather than trying to outdo their colleagues.

The team decided, with the DON's approval, to bring ideas to the next nursing management meeting of how they could develop more team spirit on each of their units, as well as to share their ideas so the whole nursing department could benefit.

Chris discussed involving her whole staff in the process of developing ways to increase a team spirit, emphasizing cooperation not competition, with Marie. Marie's smile seemed to Chris to be saying she was proud of her protégé. She suggested giving the staff at least one example that Chris felt would help build a team spirit, so they could both feel safe expressing their ideas, and have a better understanding of what Chris was actually asking them to do.

Chris felt excited about this new concept. Being a realistic person, though, she also knew the staff might feel a bit confused by this empowering project, while still adapting to the edicts from the CEO. She understood it would be more difficult to create an atmosphere of cooperation and a feeling of empowerment while working in a system headed by someone who did not involve the people who actually had to do the day to day work of the facility, but on whom his decisions had a major impact. She decided to focus first on how the unit staff could create a workplace where people felt enthusiastic to come, knowing they were limited to what they as a staff could do with and for each other. She thought deeply about what idea she would present as an example of how to create this positive workplace, before actually sharing the concept with the unit staff.

Chris decided she would present the idea of *win-win* to the staff as hers. She knew she would have to explain just what a win-win environment would be like and what belief would need to be embraced so the behavior would follow. She decided to give examples of what a *win-lose* situation looked like, and compare it with one where both parties went away from an interaction feeling as if they were valued, and were essentially satisfied with the result. Having spent some time practicing both how she would present the overall concept and the script she would use to share the explanation, Chris was ready to involve the unit staff.

She called another all-staff meeting, letting them know ahead of time that she would appreciate a discussion on what the staff thought would be the most important points to developing a cooperative, non-competitive team spirit on their unit. The staff seemed to Chris to be enthusiastic when they arrived. The discussion was lively, and several ideas came out of the meeting. First of all, they unanimously agreed that the idea of creating win-win situations was much better than encouraging each staff member to try to outshine the other, which often propagated cutthroat competition among people who were working together.

The next most popular idea was a need to be honest and upfront with each other. Chris did clarify, however, that she wanted people to use assertive communication, such as "I feel" statements when expressing themselves honestly with peers. Sometimes when people start to be more honest with each other, she knew, the communication could take on a blaming or critical tone, which tends to make other people defensive. Most staff members nodded when Chris encouraged assertively sharing their feelings, disagreements, etc. while a few did look bewildered, especially Brenda.

Other staff members shared that it was vital for them to feel important and appreciated when they did a good job, and gave Chris suggestions how she could give them this positive feedback. Due to differences in personality styles, some staff members shared different ways they could be shown appreciation. Just as Chris had learned from her research, however, what staff really want from their supervisors—and what her team also expressed—were the needs to feel important and appreciated, and not one mentioned wanting a raise in pay.

Some staff confided it was important that when they did share, people would not laugh at their ideas, a reaction probably based on those individuals' past experiences. Chris remembered her own fears of being criticized or laughed at, so this suggestion was one she would definitely try to implement. Some staff also shared they were not comfortable with conflict, although they knew it usually exists with diverse personalities trying to work together. Chris gave those brave staff members positive acknowledgement that conflict indeed can be stressful. She then added that when diverse people work together, it is normal.

She wondered if they could see the positive side to it, such as that sometimes conflict can generate creative ideas that, if embraced, can actually improve a situation. The group became silent for a moment, but then some nodded and even smiled. After all, conflict often only came from misunderstanding, or differing beliefs or ideas. If team members could become more open to hearing others' points of view and be less reactive, many times a new idea could be beneficial to the working of the team.

Some staff, mainly the influencers, suggested they would like to get to know other members of the team more as just people. Although Chris knew people did not have to be best friends to work effectively together, she did ask the team to think of ways they could get to know each other better, with the aim of deepening the understanding of both their differences and commonalities. The people who valued security wanted to make sure they were kept up on all new information and that there were consistent ways to share important knowledge. Some of the dominant personalities wanted to develop a clear team vision delineating both team and individual goals and responsibilities. The conscientious people wanted to develop ways to track how well teamwork goals and responsibilities were actually working once they were implemented. They also stressed that once developed, these team goals and responsibilities should be communicated to new staff during orientation.

The most popular suggestion was to continue having meetings where staff could be involved in problem solving and decision making. They expressed that the best people to make many decisions regarding a unit were the people actually doing the work. Chris smiled proudly at her professional staff, and gave them immediate positive feedback for their suggestions and insights. She realized, being their leader, she would be the one who needed to help implement these suggestions in an organized way. Developing the suggestions into a shared vision reflecting team values as well as setting goals and clarifying responsibilities of both the team and individual members would be easier to accomplish due to the staff input she received. She knew the more input a team had into making decisions, the more buy-in they would have to actually implement these changes.

Chris enthusiastically took the list of her teams' suggestions to help build a cooperative group spirit to the next nursing management meeting. She was surprised that some of the other nurse managers who followed through with bringing in ideas to help build these positive teams, did not include their staff in making their lists. Some did not follow up with making a list at all, and some, like Chris, accomplished the task by involving part or all of their staff. Chris was also surprised to hear that those who did involve their staffs brought quite similar lists. The same theme, especially the two points of wanting to feel valued and appreciated, were unanimously prominent issues.

The nursing management team then began to brainstorm ways they could help their staff feel more valued and appreciated. Chris tentatively suggested they could practice with each other, as well, both to help their own team have a more proactive morale and to get feedback from each other about how the attempts felt before sharing them with the staff. The nursing management group, at least most of them, seemed energized by this proactive stance. Some verbalized they also felt disempowered over the two recent CEO decisions, as well as unappreciated, along with their professional staff.

By the nursing leaders becoming more self aware and acknowledging their feelings with other members of their leadership group, the overall feeling in the room seemed to change for Chris. She formerly had felt disillusioned when with this group, and defeated. Now the nursing leadership team seemed to take on a more positive and powerful attitude. If they could create a cooperative nursing team vision, and develop both group and individual goals and clear responsibilities with a way to track their progress, they might be able to change the culture which presently seemed to be more reactive than positive.

Chris felt proud now to be part of the nursing leadership team. Although she remained realistic, knowing they could only do so much at their level of management to actually create a positive working environment, she felt re-energized. Chris planned to bring back the idea of creating a nursing vision to the staff, and ask for their input in developing one. There was a nursing department overall mission that all direct-care employees would provide excellent patient care relative to their roles within the department. However, after creating what Chris viewed as an excellent overall list of requirements to develop a cooperative team spirit, she had confidence that their unit staff could also brainstorm great ideas to be fine tuned as a nursing vision with the other leaders and their units' staff input.

She talked with Marie to help her define clearly the difference between a mission statement and a vision statement. Marie suggested letting the staff know that the nursing department's mission statement and core competencies would be a good place to start, but that a vision statement was more future oriented. She said to describe it as a picture of what they wanted their unit and the nursing department as a whole to look like with a framework for strategic planning in order to get to the aspirations. "While it is not an actual plan for getting there, it does help remind us what we are trying to build," Marie shared. Chris was not too clear yet as to just how to define a vision statement, nor how to then engage her unit staff in trying to develop at least a basic outline of one that embraced their most important values.

Marie suggested Chris try using a formula that included:

1. A time frame, such as within _____ years.
2. Our nursing department will become known as the most _____ in our field.
3. Increasing patient and staff satisfaction to _____.

4. And the community will say_____ about us.

Marie made sure to let Chris know this was just a rough outline, but it should be a good starting point for the staff. Chris presented the outline at her next all-staff meeting and received many positive ideas. While the draft mission statement was a diamond in the rough, the staff was sure they could make something special happen in as little as two years. They suggested the department could be known as the most patient friendly, as well as highly skilled, in its field. They felt the department could increase both patient and staff satisfaction to a stellar level and that the community would say their hospital was the premier health care environment.

Chris brought her staff's input back to the next nursing leadership meeting to be included for discussion with the rest of the department, and to help polish their joint vision statement. The DON smiled approvingly at Chris, which made Chris feel even more enthusiastic about her management work.

What did Chris learn about creating a team spirit?

1. A middle manager in nursing actually was leading three teams, not just one, and often the shifts competed with each other rather than creating a harmonious cooperative spirit.
2. Competition between teams (shifts) and among team members often creates an angry, tension-filled working environment.
3. Helping all shifts feel more valued and having their unique contributions acknowledged can help create a healthy, cooperative work place.
4. Backbiting can be an indication of one team member feeling the need to win and thereby creating win-lose working relationships.
5. Sometimes backbiting behavior, which can tear shifts apart, can also be attributed to the backbiting bully feeling that she/he is less liked than her "competitor".
6. Developing creative ways to help staff both give and get acknowledgment for their valuable contributions can help build a positive, cooperative team spirit. Peers, for example, can have some fun engaging in the quarter system and

focusing on another's "greatness" rather than trying to outdo that person.

7. Brainstorming as both a unit and a leadership group is a powerful tool to help get a team to share their ideas and feel empowered, as well as to buy-in to solutions.

8. Showing respect for each team member's ideas, even if they are way out of the box, is paramount. No one likes to be laughed at or have their input be disrespected.

9. As a leader, it is important to both encourage the quieter members to share and give positive acknowledgement to individuals for their input.

10. Making a list of ways to create a win-win cooperative team spirit, based on the input from the staff, reflects the teams' values.

11. Full staff meetings held regularly get continuing input from all three shifts and help the members become more bonded, even though some diverse personalities may never be "friends".

12. Some team members in the leadership group, for example, may not be as invested as others. As in any group of people, there are those who are more proactive and better with follow-through than others.

13. By becoming more self aware and acknowledging their own feelings, the leadership group themselves can create a healthier, more supportive environment which they can then bring back to their units.

14. Developing a group vision is a powerful way to help a whole team work together to cooperatively create a more dynamic future for their department.

(To obtain more information about developing cooperative teams and dealing with other current leadership challenges/issues, and to discover how to receive *Nurse Career Success Tips* for free, visit: *www.NurseCareerSuccess. com.*)

CHAPTER ELEVEN

Mentor, Mentor, Mentor

Chris was proud of the work she and her teams accomplished creating a vision for the future of the nursing department. She also felt more positive and calmer coming to work each morning. While there were still issues she knew were out of her control, such as not being sure what the CEO might decide to do next that would make an impact on her unit, she felt in general more on top of things in her position. She became savvy enough to know that keeping a team on a positive track was just as hard at times as beginning on the path. It would require Chris to be vigilant and available both professionally and, if needed, as an emotional support to her staff when they experienced tough times. Chris would need to constantly both self and team assess. Being the leader for her unit, it was important to maintain both a professional and warm/caring attitude while trouble shooting for possible staff conflicts or other potential problems.

Chris was glad she had Marie as her loyal mentor. She looked back over her first year in leadership and realized how vital Marie's role was in helping her to succeed. She felt lucky to have such a knowledgeable and caring person to go to when she had challenges and was not sure how to handle the situations. Chris thought about a time in the past when she had not had a positive and supportive guide. She physically shuddered when remembering how alone she had felt in those days. She recalled one day when she had come to work with a killer headache, dragging herself in despite wanting to just stay at home under the covers. In this other high responsibility job, she had been expected to "make" peers be on time with their paperwork, but with no formal title or authority. To make matters worse, that group of people had worked more like just a "bunch" than a team. They had not liked one another much, it seemed, and had no respect for a "newby" quality assurance person telling them anything. That group had worked like a dysfunctional family for several years together. Backbiting and gossip had run rampant.

People in that group had either smiled in her face then criticized her behind her back, or had made sarcastic remarks. When confronted, those passive aggressive sarcastic style personalities had made it sound as if Chris were too sensitive. She hadn't even begun to know how to make the backbiters talk to her rather than about her. Just the thought of dealing with that group of people, with no positive mentor to help her, still made her shudder.

Marie was a rock for Chris to lean on when she needed her, and was also her cheerleader when she was able to accomplish a milestone or even one small step toward successfully completing her middle management first year's journey. Her emotional maturity and greater experience seemed to be shared selflessly. The now seasoned nurse manager was especially thankful for Marie because, even though Chris' success might make the DON look good, it really would have no impact on the evening nursing supervisor. Thinking about Marie's selfless giving, her offers of helpful ideas, wisdom and aid to help Chris set high self expectations and succeed in meeting them, made Chris smile gratefully. She realized that part of her role, also, would be ongoing mentoring of the unit staff. Brenda might need the most attention, but quieter staff members often have issues they don't express. Unless she was willing to attend to their ongoing professional and sometimes even personal needs, these staff members would not be willing or able to give their best. She also knew she would have to approach the various personality styles in different ways to help inspire her mentees to do their best work.

In order to meet the mentoring needs of her staff, Chris decided first to remember what motivates each personality style.

The dominant style people were dynamic problem solvers, and might want to rush to action without really looking at all angles and many times without considering anyone else's opinions. On the good side, they like change, which Chris knew was basically a constant in the health care field today. However, since they also have a fear of being taken advantage of, she was aware they would be the most likely to more overtly have difficulties dealing with upper management decisions, such as the two recent CEO changes. Since her D style team members had no input in deciding the recent changes, were now required to do extra work, and felt badging in was a slight to their professionalism, she realized edicts might create a more severe impact on this group. They could become more negative and/or use sarcastic or aggressive remarks, which Chris had already experienced with Darlene and Deborah.

In order to help mentor this challenging group, Chris needed to constantly monitor her own feelings and reactions so she could remain at least outwardly calm and even tempered, but firm enough so she did not appear to be a weak leader. Dominants did not seem to have much respect for a leader who was too sweet, but at the same time Chris knew she did not want her behavior to be too militaristic with them. Either extreme would make her an ineffective mentor to this group of people.

Influencers such as Ida and Irene were a challenge to mentor for another reason. They were always outwardly friendly, but you never knew what they were really thinking. That is, unless someone else told you what they were saying behind your back. She knew the reason they appeared to be "two faced" was simply that they did not want to be rejected. Also they might be the ones who would gush they were fine with a new rule, expectation, etc., then might fail to follow through and actually implement the new expectation. Since they were the least detail-oriented people on the team, paperwork or other perceived drudge work might get behind, simply because they do not value details.

In order to mentor influencers, Chris knew she would need to keep their fear of rejection in mind and give feedback gingerly, especially when it might be construed as negative. She knew she had to build a more personal bond with this group than with any other in order to create a trusting mentor relationship. She needed to encourage completing paperwork, for example, possibly by adding some humor and understanding that it *was* drudge work, but it was also essential for the team member's success. Chris also knew she needed to remember that this personality style might often agree with an earnest voice to get paperwork updated, etc., but then just pretend to go along with the goal. This group needed to get the message that direct communication was not only a good thing, but also was one way to actually ensure Chris would like them more. If they felt for even a moment that Chris would reject them, or just get upset with them for voicing their real feelings, they would immediately go back underground and backbite, and Chris was aware of this danger.

However, since Chris herself did not like criticism much, she knew that people beginning to share feelings openly and honestly might come across in an accusatory or other non assertive way. Therefore she would have to be patient with them until they could both feel comfortable sharing their feelings openly and do so in a nonjudgmental manner. She decided part of her mentoring process would be to teach assertiveness skills to her staff.

Steadiness people, such as Stan, would listen intently and generally be compliant to whatever Chris or other people in authority would ask of them. She knew she could count on their people skills to help reconcile conflicts with staff as well. However, the nurse manager also knew this group of people would need more time to adjust to changes, and that they sometimes held grudges, silently. This type of personality would be sensitive to criticism, since they fear the loss of their security. One area they might need mentoring in would be helping set their priorities. Infusing a sense of humor into suggesting ways for these people to organize their day in order to get the most important tasks done first, would be one way Chris could mentor this group positively.

Compliance people, like Connie, were usually the most quiet members. Since they are analytical, careful and precise, and work at high personal standards, they also make decisions slowly and carefully, based on facts. They would be the most deadpan looking people in the room when a change is introduced. After they have all the facts, they are often good gate keepers to keep the more dynamic part of the team from moving forward too fast, without taking certain aspects into consideration first. Chris knew they sometimes were too fact oriented and often came across as critical of new ideas or changes. To mentor this group of people she would need to listen to what they were really saying rather than how they might be saying it. The trick, she knew, since they feared criticism themselves, was not to get defensive when feedback from a compliance person might seem to shoot down one of her ideas.

Chris knew ongoing mentoring was one of her most important roles as a modern middle manager. She had read some books about emotional intelligence, Goleman (2004) that seemed to indicate that middle managers needed to have high emotional intelligence ratios. It made sense to her since she really was the person who truly was the one in the middle. She had to carry out changes she might not agree with from upper management, be part of a peer group that could either help set higher standards for nursing care or turn into a haven for complaints and become stuck, and be the role model as well as the perceived authority figure on her unit. This trio of roles had to be balanced.

She identified each team as a dynamic open system, ever adapting to constant change. She had a pivotal role on her unit, but found through the recent project of helping to develop a vision for the future of her department that her role could be transforming in at least two of the three groups to which she belonged. Since the mentoring role included being a good role model, she in effect could act as one, both on her unit and within the leadership group. She realized her consistent, professional but warm communication style could be very influential creating a healing environment for their patients and a warm and caring working environment as well.

What did Chris learn about mentoring?

1. Keeping a team on a positive track required continual vigilance. Sometimes it was just as hard to stay on track as it was to develop it.
2. She needed to constantly assess both herself and the team. On her part she wanted to maintain a professional and warm/caring attitude, while at the same time trouble shooting for any staff conflicts that might need her intervention.
3. Chris continued to develop a trusting relationship with her own mentor, Marie, and realized this important support person had helped her succeed through her first year as a nurse manager.
4. She remembered trying to go it alone in a high-responsibility but low-authority job, working with a "bunch" rather than team of people. It had affected her physical health to try to deal positively within a system where backbiting and gossip prevailed. By comparison, she felt glad in her present position to have Marie as her mentor for support.
5. Chris learned mentoring different personality styles would take some finesse. What motivated one style would not necessarily engage the others:

a. Dominants love to problem-solve but fear others might take advantage of them. They are more likely to be either aggressive or passive aggressive communicating when they are dissatisfied. To mentor this group, Chris knew she had to maintain a professional but respectful attitude and an even-tempered demeanor.

b. Influencers want to be liked. They are usually very friendly on the surface and outgoing in their communication, but often are the most likely to backbite or gossip. That way they feel they can keep up the relationship while expressing their displeasure about something, even though backbiting behavior actually undermines a good relationship. To mentor this type of personality, Chris knew she had to connect more personally with them, and create a bond where they could feel safe to express their real feelings and not risk rejection (their biggest fear).

c. Steadiness people, she knew, would usually be compliant with changes she asked of them due to their respect for authority. She could also engage them to help reconcile conflicts with other staff. To mentor them, she would need to give them time to adjust to changes and help them to verbalize any resentments, otherwise they might hold grudges. Since they fear loss of security, and are sensitive to criticism, Chris would need to be especially gentle giving this group of people constructive feedback when she needed to help them prioritize, for example. Humor often worked, she discovered.

d. Compliance people presented a different challenge. Since they are the most quiet in a room, usually, and often appear emotionless when a change is introduced, she knew she would have to take some individual time to get them to share their feelings. She would also need to accept that, since they make decisions based on facts and are not especially "people" people, their feedback might come across as critical of new ideas. To mentor this group, therefore, Chris would need to be especially careful not to respond in a defensive way to them, and to keep her own emotional reactions to a minimum.

6. In order to be an effective middle manager, she would need to continually develop her own emotional intelligence (Goleman 2004) to a high degree. Being the manager truly in the middle, she had to carry out decisions she might not agree with from upper management; be part of a peer group that could either set high standards or become stuck in complaints and feelings of powerlessness; and be the perceived authority figure on her own unit. She knew this trio of roles had to be balanced and that each team would be constantly adapting to change.

7. Her mentoring role on her unit included being a good role model. She realized her own consistent professional but warm communication style could help create a positive, healing environment for patients as well as a work environment where staff would enjoy coming to their jobs.

CHAPTER TWELVE

Summary of Leadership Success Secrets

When Chris completed her first year as a nurse manager, she felt satisfied and enthusiastic about the future of both her unit staff and the nursing department. True, there was still the challenge to try to get upper management to appreciate the department's accomplishments, but that would be another story. She went over in her mind just how her choices, beliefs and her own continuing growth helped spur changes both tangible and intangible.

First, Chris chose a positive mentor in Marie. Marie was wise, caring and compassionate as well as very management/leadership savvy. She was a constant support for Chris throughout her growth into a more mature and confident nurse leader.

With Marie's guidance and using her own research, she began the tricky journey of understanding staff members' differences in order to more effectively lead all three of her teams. She purposely appeared friendly, i.e., smiling, when she greeted each staff member and sat with a open posture to help staff feel more comfortable interacting with her.

She was reminded we have two ears and only one mouth for a reason. Listening was really key to getting her staff to share their thoughts, needs, ideas and feelings. Although it seemed backwards to Chris at first, as it does to many new middle managers who think it is important to let people know who they are and what they expect, listening is the first secret to building a highly effective, cohesive and harmonious team. She realized some people might need more encouragement to speak in meetings, while others might need some help bottom lining what they had to say. Just letting someone finish their thought before responding was paramount, even if the leader wanted to share positive feedback.

Nodding or in some other way showing she understood was another way to help people share more openly, which was a challenge for Chris at times when she might not agree with what was being said. Chris also had to overcome the "super woman" belief that she should be able to fix every problem presented, because just knowing they were heard often was enough to help staff deal with a difficult situation. Since Chris tended to talk fast at times, she learned to become aware of the tone, speed and clarity of her words using a tape recorder and a mirror and consciously slowed down when needed.

Next Chris learned there were many differences within her teams. One was a generational difference. She had all four generations working together and each had a different belief about work. She was surprised by her research, however, finding that most culturally diverse people really had more in common than they had differences. She learned it was important to respect a person's ethnicity, religious and sexual preferences, and also their right to privacy. Marie helped Chris learn people communicate in a variety of modes, and that sometimes matching words helps create a rapport with someone who uses different sense words. Since people have varying ways to interpret the world around them, Chris realized it was easy to misinterpret messages and/or behavior. She learned to be observant on many levels while she assessed both her teams and the issues that might need to be addressed. She realized she was utilizing the first step in the nursing process—assessment--and that it was really important to assess before trying to plan, implement or evaluate any changes she might see as needed. The most challenging part of the process was self assessment. She had to ask herself which communication mode she used most, what generation she belonged to, and if she had any cultural biases.

However, early in assuming her role, Chris also had to deal with sudden changes over which she had no control, making her initiation more challenging.

The first of the two new CEO decisions did not give Chris enough time to actually plan ahead. During a change that might have created a feeling of loss to the staff, she knew she had to be cognizant that the staff might go through the grief process, which begins with shock and disbelief. Therefore, their initial reaction might be less overt.

She learned to view a potentially problematic staff member as an emotional barometer for the rest of the team, as she belonged to the personality type that showed their negative feelings openly, although sometimes either aggressively or passive-aggressively, with sarcasm, eye rolling, etc. She learned to encourage staff to share their reactions openly without fear of repercussion. Chris engaged all three shifts in the problem solving process, especially the leadership people (charge RNs). She knew she had to engage different members of the team through an understanding of their personality style's unique needs.

Chris knew giving middle managers lag time to deal with a change was ideal, but that workplace changes sometimes happen so suddenly there is little time to prepare staff for them. She was also aware the second CEO decision of badging in to work could be viewed as a blow to the staff's professionalism. Although Chris herself was not sure whether she wanted to continue to work within the organization at that time, due to the CEO's leadership style, she put the effort in to keep a neutral attitude while presenting this change to the staff. It was difficult for her because even though she was the bearer of the bad news, she actually had nothing to do with making the decision.

Chris was already wise enough to engage the support of her mentor Marie several times, both to get as much information as possible to present the new rule to staff and to help deal with her own feelings. She could then come across as more supportive of upper management to the staff despite feeling disrespected as a professional herself. She asked herself the question many new middle managers ask themselves, *Could she continue to work with this CEO's management style?* After talking with Marie, she understood that some new CEOs come into a facility feeling the need to take control and make rapid changes, especially those that might save the organization money. However, often they become less autocratic once they feel more secure in their role. She realized that both personality and leadership styles of the middle manager play a role in how well members of a team can adapt to changes. She was conscientious in presenting a united front with the DON and CEO when interacting with the staff, while at the same time being understanding of their feelings.

Chris then learned there are four distinct personality types with combinations that actually create a total of fifteen (per the DISC assessment). She was able to identify the major personality styles of several of the staff. She realized that in order to effectively lead them, she had to reach these diverse styles within the context of the group, which made communicating important information and brainstorming/problem solving more complicated. She could expect different responses based on how these diverse styles communicated verbally—or failed to communicate—when asked to share their feelings, thoughts or ideas about an issue. She also realized she needed to identify her own personality style, with her own special needs, and utilize her mentor when needed.

When dealing with an outwardly difficult personality like Darlene, Chris learned that sometimes when a qualified staff member feels passed over for a promotion, tension between that person and the person who actually was given the position was situational. When the offended party decided to leave on her own to obtain a similar leadership position outside of the organization, Chris chose to respond graciously in a supportive way, making Darlene's exit easier, graceful and mutually respectful.

When replacing an employee, especially a key leadership person such as a day charge nurse, she found out you can never be sure that just because a person interviews well they will become an asset to the team. Using behavioral interviewing can sometimes at least help a leader learn how a prospective employee problem solves, but it is no guarantee the person will turn out to be a good fit with the rest of the team.

Since personality testing was not routinely administered to prospective employees, Chris did use the various techniques described in this book to get an idea of the person's most utilized style. However, it is important to note that people in an interview situation usually put on their best faces. Sometimes savvy candidates answer every question the interviewer asks with what they think the interviewer/potential employer wants to hear, rather than being open and honest. Once hired, however, they may act quite differently.

An adjustment period should always be expected, especially when a new employee takes on a leadership role within the system. The new person may feel the need to make a good impression on the boss. However, depending on the person's communication/personality style and earlier life experiences, some may mistakenly feel that if they criticize a peer to the boss, it will make the new person look better in the supervisor's eyes. Alternatively, they may backbite a peer to create a bond. In other words, they attempt to make another look bad so by comparison they look more competent, more caring etc, while creating an alliance or an "us against them" relationship. A middle (or upper) manager who has experienced this most common type of bullying behavior, as Chris had in her past, can recognize how badly it can affect not just the target of the bully(s), but the whole team.

When our new manager needed help setting healthy communication norms, which she knew from her own experience was imperative to develop a harmonious team, she consistently would seek advice from her mentor, Marie. She also continued her own leadership education by reading books about specific issues, such as dealing with bullying behavior and various personality styles. In addition, she began to master another new, all important leadership skill, the ability to self assess. She became more able to tune into her body for cues when she felt stressed, and developed her EI (Emotional Intelligence) on a continuing basis.

Our nurse manager learned to maintain a professional affect, and not respond emotionally. Empathy was a familiar attribute to her, due to her years of caring for patients. She knew that in her role, she had to transfer this empathy to dealing with difficult situations like staff conflicts, potential or actual bullying behavior, etc., in order to get each involved staff members' interpretations of what had occurred and to intervene effectively. She realized that to ensure healthy communication/behaviors within her team, norms would need to be both developed and bought into by the staff. She again worked with her mentor for pre-planning before actually engaging the team in problem solving to develop them.

She learned that building a cohesive team and healthy work environment was quite involved. First it was vital to meet the needs of each team member to feel valued, recognized and respected. Then it was important to stress cooperation and not competition within the team, to help reduce staff conflicts. Clearly stating behavioral/communication expectations through creating a list of norms, developed by the group, could help the team both create and buy into a healthy work environment. She learned using a democratic leadership style facilitates getting staff input because it is respectful of both the team's and each member's values and lets them know they are also valued as people.

Once team behavioral/communication norms are set, it is important, she found, to remind staff that it is everybody's responsibility to ensure the harmony of the team is maintained. It is not just the leader's job. In addition, it is paramount that new employees are informed of acceptable behavioral norms during their orientation. A good orientation can help ensure the new person's general acceptance by the team, as well. However, sometimes there are a few staff members who either can't or won't change their behavior. Often they will leave a team that is passionately committed to healthy respectful interactions, however. This seems to be especially true, when a passive aggressive bully gets caught in an untruth or in some other way sullying a colleague's reputation.

Chris learned to constantly be vigilant, especially during the "honeymoon" phase after a change. Depending upon the personality/communication styles of some staff, they may be just naturally slower to make changes than other staff. Also, some may have delayed emotional responses to some more unpopular changes. Using the democratic leadership style most often, Chris found, usually helped get maximum buy-in from the staff rather than just "lip service "

Chris also continually engaged her mentor in brainstorming before planning/implementing new ideas, at least the ones over which she had some control. She learned, when asking staff to make a major shift such as creating and implementing group norms, that it is best to take your time, allowing those of the staff who were slower to open up/change to become fully engaged in the process.

Chris recognized she had to work hard to proactively deal with some management difficulties, such as dealing with the passive-aggressive style of communication, for most of her career. Stressing the positives of assertive communication without sounding critical can be challenging. However, since she knew bullies in the workplace are now the number one reason people leave even otherwise satisfying jobs, it is important to discover and quickly deal with bullying behavior before it escalates to the point that a positive team member feels the need to resign.

Chris learned that creatively engaging a complaining/backbiting bully often helps the person get the attention she may be seeking in a healthy way. For example, Chris put Brenda in charge of the quarter system team building activity to help her embrace and practice team spirit behavior. This type of engagement usually is more effective than simply setting limits on behavior that could potentially tear a team apart. However, she also knew she needed to continually monitor a potential bully's behavior, as often that person's response to stress might include slipping back into old familiar behavior patterns.

She learned that part of a new manager's development was to continually go deeper into self assessment, knowing that she worked in an open system. The team and Chris would need to continually adapt to changes. A difficult pill to swallow, but nonetheless reality, was also that some things are out of a middle manager's control. Chris learned that she at times had to help her staff adjust to new decisions/rules, etc. that she had little or no input into making, and might not even agree with on a personal level.

The understanding that a middle manager is truly the leader in the middle was a sobering one for her. Some leaders, such as Chris with a high D personality style, take the need to succeed, coupled with not always being able to be in control of situations, too seriously.

To help decrease stress in both herself and her team, therefore, Chris had to learn to consciously enjoy the present moment. Being a worry wart and focusing on the what-ifs, Chris concluded, robbed her of needed energy. It also made it more difficult to focus on imminent issues, even those over which she had some control. Chris identified her worrying pattern as one learned in childhood from her earliest role model—her mother. Ingrained beliefs and automatic reactions are often more challenging because they have been around for so many years. Chris also identified that, when she felt compelled to do something, she used the "stiff upper lip" approach. She learned that having a bit of fun or just lightening up her attitude often made a stressful situation more palatable.

Adding a positive attitude, such as remembering to greet each staff member with a smile, giving positive feedback immediately for witnessed extra effort or just making good eye contact, could change the atmosphere on a unit or in a meeting.

She vowed to interject her good sense of humor to help decrease the drudgery of doing paperwork, etc. She also realized that, as the recognized unit leader, if her outward demeanor in general remained calm even amidst disruptions, the staff would tend to respond in kind to her mood, thereby helping to maintain a more peaceful ambience for the patients.

In nurse management meetings, she made the suggestion that the team focus on issues over which they had some control, rather than spending time discussing the two unpopular decisions the CEO made, in order to create a more proactive team. She realized it only took one positive person to influence not just the people she supervised, but peers as well.

To more effectively manage her own stress, Chris made a choice to use several stress management techniques. She would share a gratefulness prayer with her husband before bed to focus on what was going well in their lives. She would practice deep breathing exercises every day and spend twenty to thirty minutes at least every other day engaging in an enjoyable aerobic exercise with a buddy to help her stay motivated. She planned at least one couples fun time with her husband, as well as some alone time every week. Chris pre-planned meals so she could include the basic food groups. She journaled her feelings, ideas and wants every morning to help get in touch with her inner self, problem solve more creatively and practice not having to do everything (grammar, spelling etc.) perfectly. She found that once she filled herself up emotionally and spiritually and fueled her body effectively to help tone up her heart and other muscles, she felt less stressed and had more energy and enthusiasm for her job.

Chris also became more acutely aware that she actually led three separate teams in her role as nurse manager. She understood competition between the shifts and among team members often created an angry, tension filled work environment. By ensuring all shifts felt continually valued and that their unique contributions were quickly acknowledged, she could help create a more stress free, healthy and cooperative workplace. She identified backbiting behavior as an indication that one team member may have a need to win but in the process actually creates a win-lose working relationship with another. In the long run, however, it actually creates a lose-lose situation due to the stress this ongoing behavior causes. She realized that some backbiters might feel less liked by their supervisor than their competitor. Therefore, developing creative ways such as the quarter system and encouraging its use is one way to help staff both give and get acknowledgment for their "greatness." This type of creative team building helps establish a mutually supportive team spirit, which in turn will help decrease team stress. In other words, using a fun activity such as giving a peer a quarter to acknowledge their extra effort honors each member, rather than encouraging each member to try to outdo the others.

Using brainstorming both at the unit level and within the nursing leadership group was a tool Chris learned could help participants feel more empowered and get the whole group to buy in more easily to solutions. She became more and more skilled at getting team input on her unit, making sure to respect each team member's ideas even if some of them seemed way out of the box. After all, no one likes to be laughed at. She became more adept at helping quieter staff share their ideas by creating this safe environment and positively acknowledging their efforts. She made a list of win-win ways to create a cooperative team spirit, reflecting the teams' input and values.

In order to continue to create a vibrant team, she began regular full staff meetings. These meetings helped both to ensure she was able to get continuing input from all three of the teams, and to help the whole staff to become more bonded. Of course, she was aware that certain personality types may never actually become friends with some others.

She became more realistic that some team members may be more invested than others. Different team members might be more proactive or better at follow through, while others were better at coming up with creative ideas. She learned who to give what type of project to, for example, so the team member would be most likely to succeed.

By becoming continually more self aware and able to acknowledge her own feelings, as well as encouraging her nurse manager peers to engage in self assessment and healthy communication, Chris became a catalyst to developing the EI of the whole nursing management team. This team leadership development could then potentially spread like a "good virus" to each leader's unit, strengthening the nursing department as a whole. Developing a departmental/group vision was another powerful way Chris discovered to get a whole team to cooperatively create a more dynamic future for their department.

Once a team is on a positive track, Chris found that continued vigilance was needed to help it stay on track. To do so effectively, she needed to constantly assess both herself and her team. On her part she continued to work to maintain a professional and warm/caring attitude, but at the same time trouble shoot for any staff conflicts that might need her intervention. In order to help ensure her success, especially in her first year as a middle manager, she continued to develop a trusting relationship with her mentor, Marie. In her past, Chris had experienced going it alone, attempting to deal with a high-responsibility but relatively low-authority job, dealing with a bunch of diverse personalities who didn't get along and who talked about her badly behind her back. With no support person in that job, her health was adversely affected and she felt at great risk for career failure as well.

Actively developing a relationship with her mentor helped Chris deal effectively with challenging staff behaviors and personalities. Discussing team building issues, ideas and ways to engage the work group in creating positive solutions with Marie made dealing with them much less stressful. Continuing her education through reading books on EI (Emotional Intelligence), bullying, team building, etc., gave her creative ideas and sometimes helped guide her. Self assessing continually as well as assessing the team's needs, etc., on an ongoing basis helped sharpen Chris' EI. Goleman (2004) says in his book, *Primal Leadership*, that middle managers were rated in general as highest in EI, and it made sense to Chris that the more she developed her own EI, the more successful she would be in her position. Lastly, Chris learned that being a good role model was imperative. She made a daily effort to be consistently professional but warm when communicating, which helped to create a positive healing environment for patients as well as a unit where staff could enjoy doing their best work.

Conclusion

In conclusion, the first year of a middle manager's job is the most stressful. Our example, Chris, went through several challenges including moving too fast during her first few days, identifying staff differences that made an impact on how they responded to new leaders, changes, etc., and needing to reach out to a positive mentor/coach to help her become successful. While challenges in the form of continual changes requiring staff adaptation will always exist for a "manager in the middle," Chris learned several techniques to help her team adapt to them in a positive way. She also learned she needed to continually assess both her own reactions, feelings, etc. as well as her team's responses.

In addition, she found ways to help empower herself and the teams she supervised. Chris even gained some ideas how her microcosmic healthy unit work environment might become a role model for the full management team to incorporate facility-wide. Therefore, even subordinates to both the DON and CEO, who could demonstrate with facts that what they did created a dramatic impact, could influence the upper management to incorporate their strategies. For example, in the nursing field, some ways to prove a leader is effective is to note decreases in staff turnover and sick call-offs. Simultaneously reporting more positive patient satisfaction surveys, especially in the areas of how cared about the patients feel and how much they trust the nursing staff, can be a powerful indicator of leadership success. If she could show the upper management how a more democratic and visionary style of leadership could also positively affect the bottom line and even be effective as an internal marketing tool, even the CEO might take notice.

The possibility for this more positive future for not just her unit but for the facility as a whole was brightened when the other nurse managers and their staffs helped create a dynamic vision statement for their department. It is much easier to realize the ideal, she found, if you have an idea of where you want to go, even if you don't have a specific roadmap to get there yet. However, Chris was enthusiastic about starting her second year as a nurse manager now, with all the possibilities it could bring.

Chris, of course, was one of the lucky few who could depend on a supportive, knowledgeable and trustworthy mentor/coach. Many new female managers, and not just in the nursing field, feel they need to go it alone. Should you know of anyone who does not have a good mentor/coach, tell them not to be discouraged. This salty old supervisor offers several tools to help you deal with specific leadership challenges, including bullying behavior, stress management, building cooperative and not competitive teams, and other current leadership challenges. You can obtain my free report on creating a bully free work environment, *How to Beat Bully Behavior,* and receive *Nurse Career Success Tips* from my website: *www. NurseCareerSuccess.com.* You can follow me on Twitter at: *nursecareersucc.* I can be reached for questions, etc. at: *nursecareersuccess@rtconnect.net.* Let your leadership development journey be a pleasant and rewarding one!

References

Davenport, Noa, PhD, et al. 2005. *Mobbing, Emotional Abuse in the American Workplace.* Colins, Iowa: Civil Society Publishing.

Forrest Gump Movie Quotes: 1994, p.1

Gerber, Michael 1995. *The E-myth Revisited.* N.Y: Harper Collins Publishing, Inc.

Goleman, Daniel, et al. 2004. *Primal Leadership, Learning to Lead with Emotional Intelligence.* Boston, Mass: Harvard Business School Press.

Institute for Motivational Living. 2009. *Disc Profile Characteristics,* p.1-6.

Laborde, Genie Z. 1984. *Influencing with Integrity, Management Skills for Communication and Negotiation.* Palo Alto, CA: Syntony Inc. Publishing Company.

McClure, Valerie. 2007. *DISC Classic 2.0 report for Helen Thamm*, ALD, Inc.: Inscape Publishing p. 1-23, as part of the: *Disc Assessment Minicourse, Career Coach Institute, 2007.*

Niebuhr, Reinhold. *Serenity Prayer,* 1943.

Schneider, Ray. *Four Generations: One Workforce. 9/17/2010 Border Stylo Blog.*

Sharma, Manjula. *Nursing Process.* Express Healthcare Management Newsletter, 1/31/2004, p. 1-2

Thamm, Helen M. APRN, CPC. 2009. *Nursing Leadership Challenges Survey.*

Vidal, Michael. *Active Listening Skills in Problem Solving Methods.* Prosolva Theoretical Backgrounds Article No. 15, 5/6/2008, p 1-4.